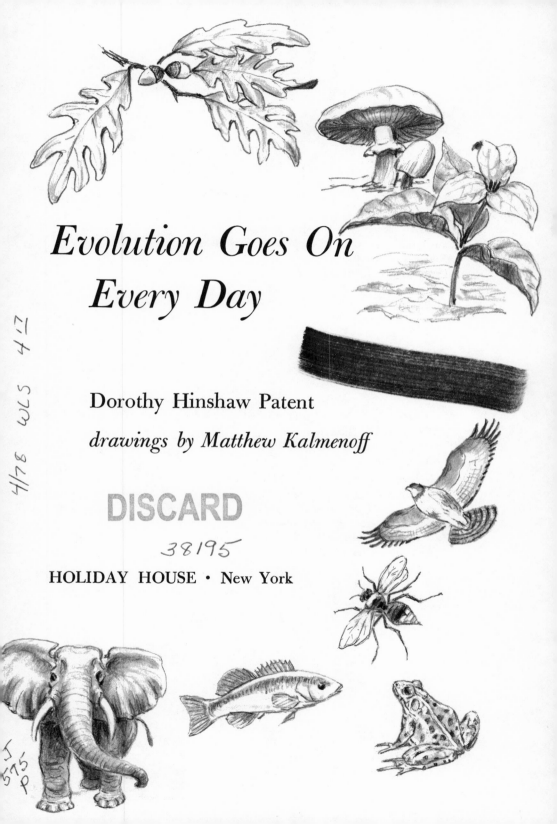

Evolution Goes On Every Day

Dorothy Hinshaw Patent

drawings by Matthew Kalmenoff

HOLIDAY HOUSE • New York

Library of Congress Cataloging in Publication Data

Patent, Dorothy Hinshaw.
  Evolution goes on every day.
  Bibliography: p. 147

  Includes index.
  SUMMARY: Describes some specific evolutionary changes occurring
in certain plant and animal species today and generally discusses genetic
mechanisms including DNA, mutations, and cloning.
    1. Evolution—Juvenile literature. [1. Evolution. 2. Genetics]
I. Kalmenoff, Matthew. II. Title.
QH367.1.P37   575   76-50525
ISBN 0-8234-0297-5

FOR MARY ELLEN,
*who has given me so much help
and encouragement with my writing*

Contents

1

The Idea of Evolution

What does evolution make you think of? Do you imagine huge, hungry dinosaurs crashing through forests of weird ancient plants? Do you see strange flying lizards swoop down to snatch up tiny furry creatures? Or do you try to cope with the mixed-up notion that monkeys changed by some mysterious process into humans?

People tend to think of evolution as a vague occurrence of long ago. Fish came into being, changed slowly into amphibians, then reptiles came along. Dinosaurs ruled the earth and became extinct, while mammals developed and gradually climbed the "evolutionary ladder" leading to human beings. While such past evolutionary developments can be documented, the process continues today, for evolution is really a basic quality of living things. It has always affected life on earth and will continue to do so as long as there is life.

Evolution proceeds around us every day, every minute, although it is usually too slow for us to see. As living things go through the cycle of life and death, successful ones leave offspring which carry along their parents' traits, but the lines of unsuccessful ones soon die out. Many familiar organisms around you are fine examples of recent and ongoing evolutionary change. The dandelions in your lawn, the house sparrows nesting under your roof, as well as the germs which make you sick—such common organisms are constantly adapting to the changes in the world around them. We'll look at them and many more examples of evolution today, as well as speculate on the evolutionary possibilities of the future. Evolution is like an unfinished story. It began long ago, continues today, and will go on in the future.

Exactly what do scientists mean by "evolution"? It can be simply defined as the process by which populations of living things change, through many generations. Although the great nineteenth-century biologists Charles Darwin and Alfred Russel Wallace put together the theory which is still the backbone of evolutionary biology, ideas of evolution have been around for a long time.

Permanence Versus Change

The essence of evolution is change, and we can trace the history of evolutionary ideas beginning with ancient Greek philosophers. From that day to this, there have been two opposing ideas of the world. One says that the world is static and unchanging, while the other says that change is a deep-down characteristic of things.

One of the earliest Greek philosophers, Anaximander, believed in change. Worlds evolved and so, he felt, must life. Living things, in his mind, arose from water as the sun evaporated it, and different kinds of organisms arose from simpler forms. He even believed that humans, and other animals, descended from fish.

Other philosophers, such as Plato, saw the world in terms of ideal forms that never changed. Visible variations were merely the imperfect expression of the ideal form. His student, Aristotle, was more of a realist, and one of the earliest true scientists. Aristotle could see that some forms of life were simpler than others, and he arranged living things on a ladder of complexity, beginning with plants and ending with human beings. However, Aristotle did not believe that the various plants and animals had evolved; they just existed and were distinct from one another. Each still represented an unchanging form. These ideas of an unchanging world had tremendous influence over people's thinking in Europe and the Americas; ideas of change or evolution were much less influential than one might expect until Darwin and Wallace came along.

The idea of static forms of animals and plants was reflected later in the biological idea of species. The great eighteenth-century Swedish biologist Carl Linnaeus set out to classify living things in an orderly fashion. To him, species were clearly distinguishable and represented fixed, unchangeable organisms. This was a reasonable view, considering the limited knowledge available at the time. He gave each species a two-part Latin name. The first part, or genus name, was a more general term. The second, or species name, was specific and unique. For example, Linnaeus called the lion *Felis leo* and the tiger *Felis tigris*. Their similarities are reflected in their shared genus name, Felis. Their differences are shown by their different species names. Although our concept of species is different today, we still use Linnaeus' method of naming species.

During the early part of the nineteenth century, those who taught and wrote of a static, unchanging world were

still the most influential. However, a great deal of scientific study of geology and paleontology had been done. Fossils of many extinct creatures had been found, and the facts became more and more difficult to explain without bringing in evolutionary ideas. But old notions die hard. Some of the greatest scientists of the day were so convinced of the immutability, the unchangeability, of species that they believed great catastrophes had destroyed all living things many times during the history of the world. But each time, a Creator had repopulated the world with new and different living things. This position became increasingly absurd as more and more fossils were unearthed. The famous scientist Louis Agassiz, who made many important and lasting contributions to science, was willing to accept from 50 to 80 separate creations and extinctions of all living things during the earth's history.

Although Agassiz and others felt that species could not change, many scientists did believe in the possibility of evolution. Probably the most famous advocate of evolution at the time was the French scientist Lamarck. The idea of evolutionary change was only a small part of his complex philosophy, but it is the one part which has had any influence on history. Lamarck believed that species could change—indeed, to him the whole concept of a species was an artificial invention of the human race.

Living things, to Lamarck, changed as they went through life. Organs which were used were strengthened,

Lamarck imagined that using an organ made changes in it that could be passed on genetically to offspring. Thus he thought, for instance, that a giraffe that stretched its neck up to eat higher leaves would have young with even longer necks.

while unused organs became smaller. He felt that these changes in structure were inherited by the next generation. In this way, organisms adjusted to their environments. For example, Lamarck imagined that the long neck of the giraffe got that way because many generations of giraffes had strained to reach leaves higher up on trees, thus slowly stretching their necks. To Lamarck, living things had a sort of urge toward perfection and greater complexity. A "life force" somehow drove them to improve.

Evolution by Natural Selection

The great British naturalist Charles Darwin had a different vision of evolution. He spent many years studying fossils as well as living animals and plants before he was willing to share his theories publicly. Darwin spent 20 years completing a four-volume book on evolution and how it occurred. In June 1858, just as he was finishing this enormous project, Darwin received a paper from another English naturalist named Alfred Russel Wallace. Amazingly enough, Wallace had come to the same conclusions about evolution as Darwin had.

So on July 1, 1858, Darwin and Wallace presented their theory together to the Linnaean Society of London. Their important ideas went largely unnoticed, however, until Darwin's book *The Origin of Species* was published in 1859. The book was an immediate sell-out, and the persuasive, well documented evidence it presented forced people to take the idea of evolution seriously. Although both Darwin and Wallace recognized the mechanism of evolution, Darwin receives more credit for his clear presentation of the evidence and his detailed formulation of the theory. Darwin's greatest contributions to science were his tremendously well substantiated evidence that evolution had, in fact, occurred, and the explanation he and Wallace had formulated of how it occurred.

Their theory is called "evolution by natural selection." They noticed that plants and animals produce many more offspring than they need to in order to replace themselves. If all the descendents of a single pair of rabbits survived and reproduced, in three years there would be over 35,000 rabbits in the family. We all know this doesn't happen. Some animals are weak to start with, and others get sick and die. Predators and accidents cause deaths, while harsh winters and severe droughts also trim down the population.

Within populations of organisms, a great deal of variation exists. Anyone who has ever raised a garden or a litter of puppies knows that some individuals grow faster and become stronger than others. Variations also exist in such visible traits as size, color, length of limbs, while less obvious internal differences are present as well. Such variations are the key to evolution by natural selection.

In any particular environment, some individuals will be more successful than others. Much of their success will be based on inherited traits which they can pass on to their offspring. These more successful individuals will have a better chance of surviving to reproduce and leave more of their kind in the next generation. In this way, over many generations, organisms will become better adapted to their surroundings. This is the basic idea behind evolution by natural selection. Darwin called it "survival of the fittest," and Wallace used an almost identical phrase, although it might better be called "survival and reproduction of the fitter."

Returning to the example of the giraffe, Darwin would say that the giraffe's neck came about through natural selection. Because of variation, some early giraffe ancestors had longer necks than others. They could reach higher leaves and thus have more food available to them. This would give them a better chance of surviving and passing their inherited trait of a slightly longer neck on to their offspring. Over many generations, more and more giraffes would have longer and longer necks because long necks had been selected by competition for food. In modern terminology, we would say that the limited food supply was a "selection pressure" which led to the evolution of long necks in giraffes.

What, Really, Is Evolution?

There are some especially important facts to keep in mind from the very beginning when thinking about evolution. First, the most important thing for a species to do if it is to succeed in evolutionary terms is *to reproduce*. It doesn't matter how strong and swift a wolf is if it never produces cubs which survive. A big, healthy plant is a complete failure as a species if it cannot leave some of its own kind behind when it dies. Many of the strangest and most beautiful characteristics of living things are based on the importance of reproduction in their lives. The antlers of male deer allow them to compete with one another for mates, while the beautiful feathers of the peacock help it attract females. It is hard to imagine a world without the colorful, sweet-smelling flowers which decorate our gardens through the seasons. But flowers merely function to attract insects or other pollinators which transfer pollen from one plant to another, allowing them to produce seeds.

Second, *evolution does not necessarily mean progress.* It is natural for humans to view evolution as the process which brought us into being. We speak of the "evolutionary ladder," of humans as the "pinnacle" of evolutionary development. Even scientists use the terms "lower" for simple organisms and "higher" to specify more complex ones. But the measure of evolutionary success is not really how complicated or intelligent or beautiful an organism is, but whether or not it is able to survive today and leave offspring tomorrow. Evolutionary changes lead to adaptations to a particular environment at a particular time. Many wondrous beings such as dinosaurs are no longer with us. They were successful only in their time. They were well adapted to certain conditions, but when those conditions changed, they could not adapt. In some way they had become too specialized, not flexible enough to respond quickly to environmental changes.

Flexibility is the key to long-run evolutionary success. Many plain, unexciting beings which originated long ago are still with us today. They have been flexible enough to adapt to environmental changes through the ages. Ancient forms like the prosaic cockroach and the inconspicuous blue-green algae may not inspire awe, but they are among the most successful of nature's creations. One could perhaps even argue that such organisms, which have changed the least over the ages, are the most successful. Certainly some of these, such as bacteria and simple worms, are among our most common living things today.

The third point to keep in mind is that *chance* is a

large element in evolution. A seed which could develop into a particularly robust, healthy plant may well be eaten before it has an opportunity to grow. A potentially strong and swift infant wildcat could die because its mother was killed. Events such as floods, forest fires, and ice ages have wiped out many well adapted organisms. Therefore, when we speak of evolution, we are really talking about probabilities, not certainties. While the fitter have a better chance of leaving more offspring than the less fit, they won't all necessarily do so. A sudden change in the environment may eliminate a well adapted population or even a whole species. For example, several kinds of previously very successful Hawaiian birds were wiped out by diseases carried to the islands by introduced bird species.

Adaptation to any given environment must be a compromise. A longer neck on a giraffe may mean that it can reach food unavailable to others, thus increasing its food supply, but it also introduces problems for the giraffe. Its heart must beat more powerfully so that sufficient blood can reach its brain, and it may not be able to run as fast as its shorter-necked companions. This is why it is better to speak of survival of the fitter rather than of the fittest, since fitness is always a compromise, and what is fit today may be less fit tomorrow. The Hawaiian birds were very fit until new diseases were brought in by other kinds of birds. Since they were completely susceptible to those illnesses, their fitness dropped to zero and they became extinct.

How Traits Are Inherited

When Darwin worked on the theory of evolution by natural selection, he did not know how variability arose, and he did not know how it was passed from one generation to the next. It is to Darwin's credit that, despite this great handicap, he was able to develop the theory which stands up well even today. In his later years he did include in his writings a belief—erroneous—in inheritance of acquired characteristics, but it was only a minor part of his theory.

To understand modern evolutionary ideas, however, some knowledge of genetics, the science of heredity, is necessary. Although the study of genetics can become extremely complicated, a brief introduction to it should give enough information to understand the evolutionary ideas and examples in this book.

Genetics actually originated during the time when Darwin and Wallace were actively publishing their views on evolution. An Austrian monk named Gregor Mendel performed experiments crossing sweet peas with different traits. He worked out the basic laws of heredity. However, his single paper, published in 1865, went unnoticed for 35 years. In 1900 three European scientists independently rediscovered Mendel's laws, and the science of genetics was born.

Since then, we have learned a tremendous amount about heredity. We even understand its basic chemistry (see Chapter 5). Each cell of a plant or animal has a central part called the nucleus, which is separated from the rest of the cell by a surrounding membrane which temporarily disappears during cell division. The nucleus is the center of the cell's activities, directing them by chemical "messages" which are sent from the nucleus into the cytoplasm of the cell through tiny holes, or pores, in the nuclear membrane.

When the cell divides to form two new cells, the nucleus divides as well. Just before and during cell division, generally rod-shaped structures called chromosomes can be seen in the nucleus. Each chromosome doubles before cell division, and one copy goes to each of the two new cells which form. Therefore, each cell of any organism has one copy of each kind of chromosome. An identical set of chromosomes is found in each cell.

The Powerful Genes

Geneticists have learned that the chromosomes carry almost all the instructions which determine the inherited traits of the organism (in some organisms a few genetic characters are carried by structures outside the nucleus). The instruction elements are called genes. Each has its own effect or effects on the animal or plant. Genes contain a code which "tells" the cell to make certain chemicals which ultimately result in physical traits of the organism, such as flower color, skin color, blood type, and so forth.

When the chromosomes of a cell are stained and studied with a microscope, it becomes obvious that they come in pairs. The two chromosomes of each pair are the same size and shape. They carry genes for the same traits, arranged in the same order. But they are not identical; they may contain different versions, called alleles, of the gene in question. For example, one chromosome may carry an eye-color allele specifying blue eyes, while its mate may carry the brown-eye allele. The two members of a matched pair of chromosomes are called homologous chromosomes.

Why do plant and animal cells have paired chromosomes? They are the result of sexual reproduction; one chromosome of each pair comes from the female parent and one comes from the male parent. When cells in the repro-

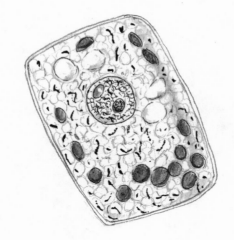

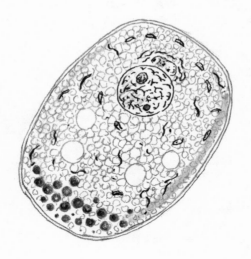

Generalized plant cell, above, and generalized animal cell, be-
low. The circular central portion is the nucleus. This contains
specialized regions called nucleoli (two are shown here) and bits
of chromatin, which contains the genetic material. The chroma-
tin forms into chromosomes when the cell divides.

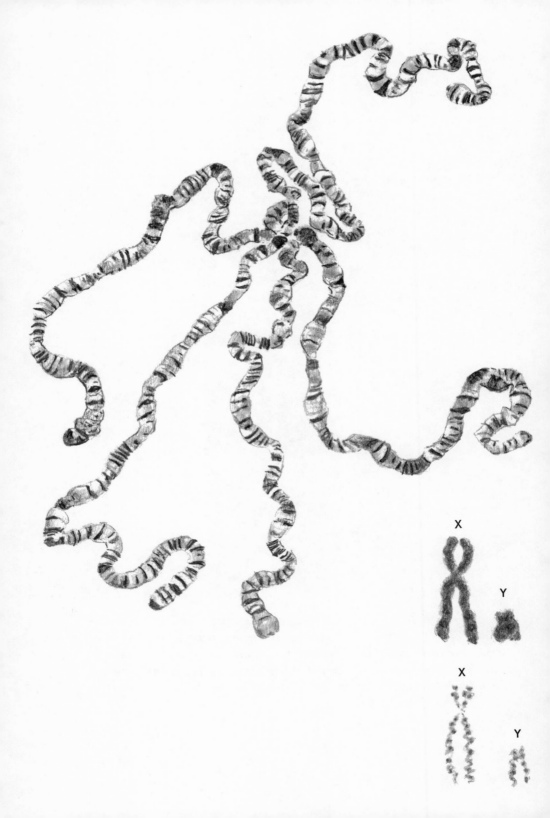

X

Y

X

Y

ductive organs divide to form eggs and sperm, the process is called meiosis. Meiosis differs from body-cell division (called mitosis). The eggs and sperm must contain half the number of chromosomes of the body cells so that when they come together at fertilization, the fertilized egg will contain the proper number of chromosomes. But each egg and sperm cell must contain one of each kind of chromosome so that the fertilized egg will have a proper set of paired chromosomes.

Meiosis assures that the egg and sperm cells will contain just one of each kind of chromosome. Meiosis consists of two cell divisions. During the first division, the homologous chromosomes line up next to each other. They have already doubled just as they do in mitosis, and the two identical strands of each chromosome can be seen under a microscope. But when the cell divides, one whole chromosome from each pair goes to each resulting cell. Each of these two cells now has half the number of chromosomes the body cells have. Then the two "daughter" cells divide again and each chromosome separates into two halves, as in mitosis.

So the result of meiosis is four cells, each with one chromosome of every pair; the result of mitotic division

The giant chromosomes from the salivary glands of the fruit fly Drosophila. The bands give clues to the location of particular genes within the chromosomes. Lower right, the sex chromosomes, X and Y, of a human male, as seen in a karyotype, or chromosome diagram made from highly magnified photomicrographs. Below them are human X and Y chromosomes after a chemical treatment that makes the coiled form of the strands clearer. Each of these coiled strands is itself made of tightly coiled double strands of DNA (the famous "double helix").

is two identical cells, each with a complete set of chromosomes. Sometimes, during the first meiotic division, while the homologous chromosomes are lined up together, two of the four strands may exchange pieces. This "crossing over" increases the mixing up of the genes, resulting in more genetic variability in the next generation.

Now let's see what all this means in terms of inheritance, using Mendel's favorite organism, the sweet pea, for an example. Sweet peas have seven pairs of chromosomes. We say, then, that the basic chromosome number, called N, of the sweet pea is seven. Each sweet pea cell, however, except for those forming eggs and pollen, has fourteen, or 2N, chromosomes in its nucleus.

One pair of chromosomes carries the gene for flower color. Mendel studied the inheritance of purple and white flowers. If a plant whose chromosomes both carry the allele for white flowers is fertilized by one whose chromosomes both carry the purple-flower allele, all the resulting seed will carry one white allele and one purple allele. This is because all the pollen from the purple-flowered plant will carry a chromosome with the allele for purple, while all the egg cells of the white-flowered plant will have a chromosome with the white allele.

What color will the flowers of the offspring of this cross be? Offhand you might expect them to be some shade of pink or lavender, a mixture of the white and purple color. But if the seeds are planted, they will all grow into purple-flowered plants. This is true even though each cell of each plant carries both the white and purple flower color alleles. The visible result of the genetic makeup of the plant, its phenotype, is purple, even though its genetic

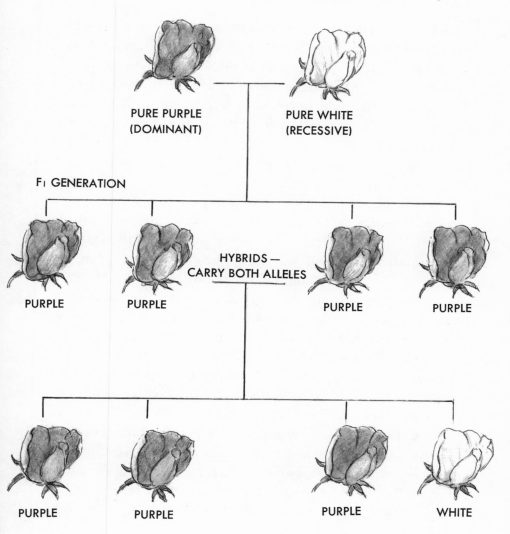

PURE PURPLE
(DOMINANT)

PURE WHITE
(RECESSIVE)

F₁ GENERATION

PURPLE

PURPLE

HYBRIDS—
CARRY BOTH ALLELES

PURPLE

PURPLE

PURPLE

PURPLE

PURPLE

WHITE

The purple allele is dominant over the white allele in this flower cross.

makeup, or genotype, is purple/white. When an allele shows its effect despite the presence of another allele, it is said to be dominant. The purple allele of the sweet pea is dominant over the white allele. And the white allele is said to be recessive to the purple one. But the white allele doesn't disappear. It just isn't expressed in the presence of the purple one.

If two of these plants which carry a purple and a white allele are then crossed and the resulting flowers are examined, about one quarter of the plants will have white flowers while the other three quarters will have purple ones. Half the pollen from one parent plant will carry the white allele and half will carry the purple one. Half the eggs will have white and half purple alleles.

At pollination, the eggs and pollen combine in a random way, resulting in about a quarter of the seed receiving a white allele from each parent, about a half getting a purple from one parent and a white from the other, and about a quarter receiving purple alleles from both parents. Only those with two white alleles will produce white flowers. These plants are said to be homozygous for the white allele. Both the homozygous purple plants (those with two purple alleles—homozygotes) and the plants with one purple and one white (heterozygotes) will have purple flowers. It is impossible to distinguish the heterozygotes from the homozygotes just by looking at them. Only by crossing them with other plants can their genotype be discovered.

Many traits are expressed in this fashion, with one allele dominant over others. There may be many alleles for any one gene (or "locus"—this word for a gene's position is often used interchangeably with the word "gene"). These may have various patterns of dominance. Sometimes, instead of one allele being dominant, the effects of the alleles do blend and produce a different phenotype. And to further complicate matters, usually more than one gene affects a particular trait, so it is often quite difficult to isolate and study the effects of a single locus.

How do all these different alleles originate? They arise through a process called mutation. Mutations occur in every generation and add to the variability upon which evolution acts. Mutation is simply a change in a gene from one allele to another. Mutations occur as mistakes during chromosome doubling while the genes are being copied (see Chapter 5). If the mistake occurs during meiosis, the new allele will be passed on to the next generation. Some mutations result in drastic changes, causing the death of the organism, while others lead to very minor differences. Some birth defects in humans may result from a mutation in the genes of one of the parents.

A particular kind of dominant dwafism is known to occur in one out of every 50,000 or so births to parents of normal height. In this case, a mutation occurred during the production of sperm in the father or during formation of the egg cell in the mother. If the dwarf grows up, marries a person of normal height and has children, half of them will be dwarfs, because each child has a 50 per cent chance of inheriting the dwarf gene from its parent.

Most characteristics of animals and plants are affected by more than one gene, and the organism is influenced by the conditions surrounding it as it grows. The developed result of heredity, the adult organism, is formed by a very complicated interaction of its many genes with one another and with the environment. In order to realize just what goes on in evolution, we're forced to simplify matters and consider just one or a few factors at a time. But we should always keep the complicated nature of heredity and of environment in the back of our minds as we try to understand the dynamic, interwoven nature of the living world around us.

2
Evolution Is Change

Through evolution, living things become changed in their structure or behavior and so become better suited to the other animals or plants, the soil, the terrain, the water, the air, the temperature and weather around them—in short, their environment. During the early history of life on the earth, these changes resulted in the development of very different kinds of living things. The variety of life around us today is tremendous. There are hundreds of thousands of different species of organisms alive today, and even more extinct species. They range from tiny single-celled bacteria to elephants and redwoods with millions and millions of cells. The greatest evolutionary changes, which led to the major groups of plants and animals, occurred millions of years ago.

Less dramatic but just as interesting evolutionary changes are going on today. They fall into two categories. First of all, changes occur with time within one species. Second, new species are still being formed. A species can be called a population of organisms which are able to breed with one another in the wild. Individuals of one species do not normally mate with individuals of another. Coyotes and wolves may be found in the same area, but they remain separate. Some species can breed with one another, forming hybrids, but usually their offspring don't survive well or cannot themselves reproduce. Horses and donkeys are separate species. A male donkey can easily mate with a mare, producing a strong and useful mule. But mules are sterile; they cannot produce offspring.

How are new species formed? Scientists generally agree that there must be a period of geographical isolation—say on two sides of an impassable river—before two populations of one species can become different enough to begin forming new species. This process is called speciation. As long as the two populations can breed together, they will keep exchanging genes and remain similar. But if they become physically separated, each can evolve in somewhat different directions. If they remain separated long enough, they change so much that interbreeding becomes difficult or impossible. Then, if they come back into contact again, they will remain as two different species, each changing over the thousands and millions of years in its own way.

On a large scale, the effects of geographical isolation can be seen in the related animals of different continents. If we look at present-day African animals and compare them to South American ones, we see many differences. Cats are found on both continents, but lions and leopards are very different from jaguars and ocelots. Both continents have monkeys as well, but there are many very important differences between New World and Old World kinds.

The Secrets of Drosophila

Since animals on these two continents have been evolving separately for a long time, they have formed quite distinct species. But often the visible differences between species, especially recently formed ones, can be very slight. Among organisms in which we can see evolution in action today, fruit flies (Drosophila) are some of the most instructive. These tiny, dull-looking creatures have been very important to biologists for many years. They have been used in the laboratory to study the mechanisms of heredity, and wild species have been used in many genetic and evolutionary studies.

By collecting wild flies of closely related species and bringing them into the laboratory, scientists have made some interesting discoveries about speciation. In several cases, fruit flies which look identical to the casual eye actually belong to different species. In some cases, the females of one kind refuse to mate with males of the other. This makes them reproductively isolated and, therefore, separate species. In other cases, the flies will breed in the laboratory, even if not in nature, but their offspring are not fertile. One cross between closely related species of fruit flies results in fertile females and sterile males. The hybrid females can breed with either parent species, but many of their male offspring are sterile.

Recently a population of one kind of fruit fly was found which is almost certainly in the earliest stages of evolving into a new species. When collections of fruit flies were made in Colombia, South America, in 1955 and 1956, no specimens of this species were found. In 1960 they began to

appear in traps in the city of Bogotá, and by 1962 they were more common there. Since the nearest population of that species was 1500 miles away in Guatemala, it is probable that the flies were introduced accidentally by humans.

In any case, they found an environment to which they were already quite suited and multiplied rapidly. In 1967 a scientist collected flies of this species in Bogotá and took them to the laboratory to compare them with others of their kind. To his surprise, he found that the Bogotá flies, although isolated from other populations for no more than 10 years, were already partially reproductively isolated. Although females from the Bogotá population would mate freely with outside males, the male offspring of such matings were completely sterile. It appears to be only a matter of time before the Bogotá flies evolve other differences which will set them apart as a distinct new species of fruit fly.

Once two species develop enough differences that their hybrid offspring either can't reproduce or don't survive well, the process of natural selection will operate to make interbreeding ever less likely. A female animal which mates with a male of a different species, producing sterile offspring, does not pass on her genes to future generations. Since her offspring cannot reproduce, they form an evolutionary "dead end." Therefore, whatever traits exist which allow interbreeding with other species will be eliminated from the

Drosophila, shown in its normal ("wild type") form at upper left, has yielded to scientists scores of important facts about speciation, inheritance, and mutations. The other three show wing mutations: upper right, vestigial (much reduced wings); lower left, curly (wings curled upward from body); lower right, curved (slanting away from body).

population wherever it overlaps with the other species. And any traits which prevent interbreeding will be passed on.

Two subspecies of a mouse called the California vole also appear to be on their way to becoming distinct species. The situation is remarkably similar to that in the Colombian fruit flies. If voles of the two subspecies mate, the male offspring are sterile; their bodies are unable to produce sperm. In this case, there are visible differences as well. For example, individuals of one subspecies are larger and have a more orange-colored coat. Differences also exist in skull shape and possibly in chromosomes.

As one can see, there are usually three stages in the evolution of new species. First, two populations become geographically isolated from one another so that they cannot interbreed. While they are isolated, each is evolving in its own way to survive successfully in its particular home conditions. As the generations pass, the two populations become more and more different. Then, if they should again come in contact, their hybrid offspring may in some ways be less fit than nonhybrids. This is the second stage, for now natural selection will favor members of each species which do not mate with the other species. Eventually the two kinds will become reproductively isolated, with little or no crossbreeding between them. They then enter the third stage in species evolution. Now each species will continue to evolve separately to suit its own environment.

The influence of each of the two species on the other has not completely ceased, however. If they are still very similar in their food and space requirements, they will be competing with one another for these resources. One of two things can happen in a case like this. If one species has an advantage over the other—perhaps it can reproduce faster or can survive on less food—it will eventually take over and the weaker species will become rare or extinct in that area. Or else, through natural selection, the two species move away from competition. For example, perhaps two closely related fruit fly species live in one area, and both lay their eggs on citrus fruits. But the larvae of species #1 can survive also on other kinds of fruit. Larvae of species #1 which are developing on citrus fruit are likely to be competing with species #2 larvae for food. But the #1 larvae that are on other fruits will not be competing, and therefore have a better chance to survive and reproduce themselves. Natural selection will favor flies which lay eggs on other fruits, so over generations females of species #1 will lay eggs less and less on citrus fruits. This is not because the flies "learn" to avoid citrus. It is because whatever genes determine egg-laying behavior and ability to thrive on certain fruits are being affected by natural selection.

Chance and Genetic Drift

Another factor besides natural selection can be very important in species evolution. It is called genetic drift. This is a random process. Certain traits may become somewhat frequent in a population by pure chance. For example, let's take a human population in which most people have brown eyes, but some have blue eyes. A group of six of these people go out in a small boat which gets carried far from shore and is shipwrecked on a small island. The people settle the island successfully and have no further contact with other human populations. If all six of the settlers have blue eyes, all future inhabitants of the island will be blue-eyed, too. The chances are, because of the small number of settlers, that they will be different from the parent population in other traits as well.

Such differences are called founder effects. And through genetic drift, some of these differences will become pronounced as generations pass. Let's say one woman had curly hair and all the other five people had straight hair. Among the settlers, then, only one-sixth had curly hair. But if the curly-haired woman was homozygous dominant (if she carried two copies of the dominant curly-hair gene), and had six children, while each of the other two women had only two children each, in the second generation 60 per cent of the people would have curly hair. You can see from this example that the smaller a population is, the greater part chance can play in evolutionary changes.

These chance changes due to genetic drift do not necessarily lead to new species, however. They can result in differences between populations of the same species as well, as in our human example. And once a species becomes well adapted to its own environmental niche (its environmental circumstances and living habits), it will change little except through genetic drift. Given a stable environment, such a species may remain virtually unchanged for generations. Natural selection will operate to eliminate mutations. Since the "best" genes have already become part of the "gene pool" of the species, mutations to other alleles not already present are likely to be less adaptive rather than more so.

Moths and Smoky Chimneys

But a change in the environment can lead to evolution within a species very quickly. The peppered moth of the

The peppered moth is an excellent example of present-day evolution that has been carefully observed. The dark form, below, was hard for birds to see and so increased in numbers when industrial soot blackened the tree trunks.

British Isles is a fine example of this kind of change. Before the Industrial Revolution, most peppered moths were light gray with a few black markings. Since the moths rested during the day on light-colored lichens which covered tree trunks, they were well camouflaged. An occasional peppered moth was dark in color. These dark moths were very easy for birds to see when they rested on the lichens, so they were quickly eaten. The few that existed were probably there because of mutations of a color gene to the dominant dark allele.

As the Industrial Revolution spread during the nineteenth century, however, the proportion of dark moths increased in areas near factories. Smoke blackened nearby trees, making the light moths easy for birds to see and camouflaging dark ones. In Manchester, for example, one dark moth was caught in 1848, but by 1895 about 98 per cent of the population of that heavily industrial region were dark.

Scientists have studied this example in great detail. They have trapped moths in different areas and counted the numbers of light and dark individuals. While almost all the moths in heavily industrial areas are dark, 95 per cent of those in rural areas are light. When scientists released equal numbers of light and dark moths onto tree trunks in unpolluted areas, 164 of the 190 moths caught by birds were dark ones. When the experiment was repeated in an industrial area, the opposite result was obtained; most moths found by birds were light ones, which were very conspicuous on the soot-darkened trunks. By taking collections in different areas and conducting experiments of this kind, scientists were actually able to measure the rate of evolutionary change going on in the moths right as it was happening.

They even found that in areas where factory smoke pollution was being cleaned up and lichens were taking over again, lightening tree-trunk color, the proportion of light-colored moths increased. Many other examples of this phenomenon, involving hundreds of moth species, have been reported from industrial areas in Europe and the United States.

3
Evolution Continues
Every Moment

The peppered moth is probably the best known and best documented example of the fact that evolution goes on all the time. But since it usually proceeds slowly, we can observe it only in organisms which have a relatively short generation time (the time from birth until the animal or plant reproduces). This is because evolution operates on populations, not on individuals. We must be able to record in some way changes of gene frequencies (the relative proportions of various alleles) over a number of generations to see evolution in action. This could be done easily with the peppered moth because the change involved a single gene controlling the obvious trait of color, and a new generation of moths is produced each year.

There must also be some change in the selection pressures operating on a species for us to see changes in gene frequencies other than those due to genetic drift. The blackening of the trees by industrial soot causes a change in selection pressure on moths which rest on tree trunks. Other kinds of pollution as well can result in new selection pressures. Our attempts to eliminate pests and diseases have also resulted in evolutionary changes. For example, when DDT was first introduced during World War II, it was extremely deadly to such pests as flies and mosquitos. Over the many insect generations which have passed since then, natural selection has favored individual insects that had some way of resisting the DDT. As a result, it takes more and more DDT to kill the same number of insects, and populations have evolved in some areas which are completely DDT-resistant.

We can affect the evolution of other organisms by changing their environment in other ways also. The common, annoying dandelion weed provides a fine example of this sort of evolutionary change. Dandelions are natural inhabitants of grassy fields. In undisturbed fields, many species of plants grow. All must reach high enough to get sufficient sunlight. Dandelions in this environment grow long leaves. They do not produce flowers until their second year of life. The first year, most of the plants' energy goes into making long leaves which can reach the necessary height.

Dandelions living in lawns face a very different environment. They get mowed down frequently. They may be dug out if found. Lawn dandelions have evolved to meet these challenges. They bloom only four months after germination and produce three times as many seeds as field dandelions. While the stems of field dandelion flowers are long, those of lawn dandelions may be very short and close to the ground. Field dandelions must grow many long large leaves reaching toward the sun, but lawn dandelions produce fewer, smaller leaves which tend to lie flat on the ground, where they suffer very little damage from mowing.

If one has fields or old vacant lots near home, it is easy to compare the dandelions in lawns and fields. Scientists who

Dandelions in dense fields of tall weeds must grow tall enough to get sunlight or die off. Dandelions on lawns don't need to.

did this found that 70 per cent of lawn dandelions were of the lawn type, while only 10 per cent of field dandelions were. No field-type dandelions were found in a lawn area which was often mowed, but 65 per cent of the dandelions in a nearby field were of the long-leaved type. These differences in the dandelions are inherited ones, caused by the different selection pressures in the two environments. Even when grown under identical controlled greenhouse conditions, they still remained true to type. Most seed from field dandelions produced long-leaved, slowly-reproducing plants, while lawn dandelion seeds grew into short-leaved, flatter plants which produced seeds earlier.

Natural selection is a very powerful force, for different forms of dandelions keep evolving over and over again, wherever these weeds are exposed to the differing selection pressures of field versus lawn living. The scientists who studied dandelion evolution worked in Massachusetts. One can see the same differences between field and lawn dandelions in Montana, and they can be seen in any part of the United States.

Even when selection pressures may seem slight to us, or may affect traits which we don't see as vital to survival, evolution can proceed rapidly. The common house sparrow has undergone rapid evolution in response to selection pressures which may seem to us trivial. House sparrows were introduced into eastern North America from England and Germany in 1852. They were very successful and spread their range rapidly. By 1900 they had reached as far west as Vancouver, British Columbia. In 1914 they were found in Death Valley, California, and they populated the Mexico City area by 1933.

In 1964 scientists sampled house-sparrow populations from these regions as well as other areas such as Texas, the Pacific coast, and Phoenix, Arizona. Despite the fact that there had been only 111 generations of house sparrows on this continent since they were introduced, and many fewer generations had lived in most areas, obvious differences in size and color were found between populations. Birds from the Pacific coast were dark, and Vancouver birds especially so. Desert birds were pale in color, and their body markings were less obvious. Birds from northern areas were consistently larger than birds from the desert Southwest.

These size and color differences are the same ones found among native animals with wide distribution. They probably relate to the need of warm-blooded animals for regulating body temperatures. A large, dark animal will retain body heat better than a small, pale one. Since it tends to be cold in the north, northern animals need to retain body heat more efficiently. Larger, darker animals will therefore be selected for. But southwestern deserts are hot places. Animals living there must be able to lose body heat easily, and smaller, lighter animals will have a selective advantage. Within a relatively few generations, house sparrows have evolved into local forms most suited to the environment of their homes.

Catastrophic Selection

So far we have discussed mostly gradual evolutionary changes caused by various pressures or genetic drift. More rapid and obvious changes are possible, however.

Except for evolutionary changes due in some way to

In only 111 generations, or fewer, house sparrows in the United States have changed in their characteristics. The Pacific coast sparrow, above, is larger, darker, and more strongly marked than the desert house sparrow.

human influence, most present-day evolution is occurring in response to unpredictable conditions around the edges of habitats. Each species of animal or plant can manage its life only within certain ups and downs of environmental conditions such as temperature and rainfall. Plants, since they cannot move around to look for water or protected places, are especially limited by such factors. And since the conditions at the edge of a species' range will come closest to these limits, an unusual year can wipe out an entire population of a plant species.

If some especially resistant individuals are present and survive, however, they will then have the area to themselves. Due to founder effects, as well as to their resistant abilities, the chances are that they will differ from nearby populations in at least some traits. And since their parent population was wiped out, they are at least temporarily isolated reproductively from others of their kind.

The flowering plant Clarkia provides some good examples of this kind of evolution. Many species of this pretty flower are found in California. They exist in colonies of varying size with quite well defined limits set largely by the availability of water. Since seeds are dropped close to the parent plant, each little colony tends to perpetuate itself.

Biologists studying the evolution of Clarkia have found that the more recent species tend to occupy drier areas than the species from which they arose. This finding indicates that catastrophic selection was involved in the evolution of new Clarkia species. For example, in 1949 a small colony of white flowering plants of one Clarkia species was noticed near a very large pink-flowered population. The two colonies were separated by less than ten meters (about 33 feet), but they remained the same for six years. In the winter of 1955, the rains stopped a full month earlier than in any other year, causing very dry conditions. In 1956 the white colony was very large and healthy, while only a few pink stragglers survived. By 1966 a very large area was occupied by the white-flowered race. Whether or not this situation will lead all the way to evolution of a new Clarkia species remains to be seen. But it is a good example of how one unusual year can exert strong enough selection pressure to cause a visible change in a population in just one generation.

Instant Evolution

Ordinarily, for a change such as the one described in Clarkia to result in new species' being formed, some change in the reproductive pattern must also occur. A common way for new plant species to form is through an increase in the number of chromosomes present. Because of the pairing of homologous chromosomes during meiosis, a derivative plant with a different number of chromosomes cannot produce fertile offspring if it is crossed with its parent species. For meiosis to occur successfully, each chromosome must pair with the other of its kind, so that the resulting "daughter" cells will each have the correct number of chromosomes. Thus, if a plant forms through some mistake in cell division which results in extra chromosomes, it can found a new species.

Some plant families have carried this process to extremes. The most primitive fern family has related species with chromosome numbers ranging from 120 to 630! This is probably the highest chromosome number found in plants.

Usually the chromosome numbers of such related species do not differ that drastically. One species of Clarkia which differs visibly only in petal shape has nine pairs of chromosomes instead of the eight of its closest relative. Because of that extra pair of chromosomes, hybrids between the two species are very seldom fertile.

Sometimes new species arise simply by chromosome-doubling. This has occurred often in plants. A new species of wild salsify formed in Washington State in this way. Two species of European salsify introduced into the area frequently hybridize, but the resulting plants are sterile. Because their ranges in Europe do not overlap, these species never evolved ways to prevent hybridization. In 1949 a few fertile hybrid colonies were found. These large plants possessed 12 pairs of chromosomes instead of six. Since there are two of each kind of chromosome now present, the chromosomes can pair normally during meiosis and produce normal pollen and egg cells. In only 25 years this weed has become one of the most common plants found in vacant lots in and around the city of Spokane, Washington.

Until recently, the appearance of new species by chromosome-doubling was thought to be rare in animals. But microscope studies have uncovered several "hidden" species of frogs with double the usual chromosome number. These frogs may look like their parent species, but cannot breed with them because of the different chromosome number. In some cases, the mating call of the two species differs, keeping hybridization to a minimum.

Another form of instant evolution in plants is the occurrence of self-pollination in a mutant from a cross-pollinating

This new species of wild salsify appeared through chromosome-doubling.

population. A single mutation can probably result in this change in reproductive pattern. If the mutant and its off-spring are successful, they are automatically a new species since they cannot cross with the parent species.

Such a new species was found in the plant genus Stephanomeria in the sagebrush desert of eastern Oregon. Out of a total population of about 35,000 plants of one kind, 750 were found to belong to a self-pollinating new species. The chances of this new species' surviving for long are not great, however, for it grows smaller and more slowly, and produces fewer seeds than the parent species. One other characteristic could cause it to disappear entirely in one bad year. While seeds of the parent species must freeze before they will germinate, the new species' seeds will germinate as long as it is cool and moist. This trait would be fine in a frost-free environment. But in eastern Oregon, one year with a damp fall followed by a severe cold spell could result in extinction of this little experiment of nature.

Such experiments sometimes prove successful, however. A thriving species of Stephanomeria found as a weed along roadsides and fields probably also originated from a self-pollinating mutant some time ago. This species was able to live in a different habitat from that of the original species, and now it is found from northern California to eastern Washington and Idaho.

Parthenogenetic Animal Species

New species formed by changes in mode of reproduction are less common in animals than in plants, but they do occur. There are several all-female fish "species" in Mexico which mate with males of the parental species from which the all-female species came. But through complicated cellular mechanisms, the male chromosomes are rejected and never have any effect on future generations. Scientists have even manufactured one such fish "species" in the laboratory by crossing related species.

In lizards, new species are found which do not need to mate at all to produce eggs which develop. Why these peculiar species should have formed several times in lizards is a scientific mystery. These parthenogenetic species are produced when two closely related species interbreed to form hybrids. The hybrids then mate with a parent species, producing offspring with an extra set of chromosomes. Now a new, all-female species has formed. If the new species can successfully occupy an available habitat, it will thrive. And since the females don't mate before laying their eggs, all the offspring will be exactly like their mother and one another, unless mutations occur. Interestingly enough, these parthenogenetic lizards are often found in marginal, extreme, or disturbed habitats, just as the derived species of plants are.

Right now, a parthenogenetic whiptail lizard species is continually reappearing, but it doesn't appear to be very successful. There is evidence that hybridization leading to this particular hybrid has been going on for over 125 years, but for some reason it is quite rare. Other parthenogenetic whiptails have formed by hybridization involving other parental species, however, and are very successful.

It appears that extra chromosomes increase chances of survival for some plant and animal groups in marginal habitats. Biologists disagree on the meaning of this phenomenon, but many feel that the extra chromosomes enable organisms living in such areas to carry along a greater

This is Cnemidophorus uniparens, *a desert grassland species of lizard that need not mate to produce young. There are several species of such lizards, some of them quite successful.*

variety of alleles, giving them more flexibility to meet the extreme demands of their environment.

Coevolution—First One, Then the Other

Species must adapt not only to the physical environment around them but also to one another. Much of the selection pressure on any species is due to the other living things around it. Hungry birds affect moth evolution and competing plants challenge field dandelions. Predator and prey, host and parasite affect each other's evolution enormously. If a host develops a defense against a parasite, the pressure is on the parasite to evolve a way around it. If a prey species becomes more cunning at escape, its predators must become better catchers or miss meals—perhaps enough of them to die off. This more or less simultaneous alteration is called coevolution.

The most striking examples of coevolution in action come from the interactions between insects and their food plants. Insects have one or more generations each year, and most food plants are annuals or biennials, with one generation each year or one every other year. Both the insects and their host plants can therefore evolve rapidly.

Many plants produce poisonous chemicals which protect them from hungry insects. Cabbage family plants produce mustard oil compounds which are distasteful to most insects, and sometimes poisonous. But certain insects have evolved ways to neutralize the effects of the poisons. Some, such as the common white cabbage butterfly, have gone a step further. They use the presence of mustard oil chemicals as a signal to identify a proper food plant. The same situation exists with members of the potato family. These plants, such as tobacco, potatoes, tomatoes, and eggplant, contain powerful poisons in their leaves. But a few insects, such as the tobacco hornworm and Colorado potato beetle, are immune to the toxic chemicals and thrive on food which

Plants and insects are often in an evolutionary race, so to speak, to "outwit" each other. Some plants of the cabbage family produce chemicals that repel insects, but the white cabbage butterfly has adapted to these substances and even identifies suitable food for its larvae by them.

could kill other insects. Since these plants are all cultivated and protected by humans, there is no selection pressure on the plants to evolve further defenses.

In nature, however, similar situations result in a constant evolutionary contest. A strain of insect comes along which feeds successfully on the plant. Selection pressures now favor any plants with some resistance to the insect. They will increase. Then selection pressures favor insects which can bypass the new defenses—and so forth. The coevolutionary race is an endless contest in which the balance tips first in favor of one organism and then the other. Other species affect the interaction as well. Humans are among them, as we will see later.

4
What's Next?

Whatever we may say about the apparent direction of evolution in a certain species, we cannot actually predict the outcome of the changes. Most scientific theory is based on predictions. A theory is made which predicts the outcome of experiments. If the experiments give the expected results, that is evidence that the theory may be correct.

But the study of evolution is still largely in the descriptive stage. We can look at the fossil record and study the evolutionary changes of the distant past. We can even examine more recent changes in species living today. But we have no way of predicting what sorts of evolutionary change will occur in any particular organism tomorrow or in a hundred years. So many factors affect the evolution of any living thing that it will probably never be possible to make complete and reliable predictions. The climate, the condition of other species with which it interacts, the size of its population, as well as unexpected catastrophic events, are all factors which have important influence. To further complicate matters, scientists still do not agree on the relative strengths of the various forces involved in evolutionary changes.

In order to establish itself in a new niche, a species must be able to survive there to begin with. The word "preadaptation" has been used to describe traits an organism already possesses which make it able to use a new environment. The Colorado potato beetle was not originally a pest of potatoes. It fed on a wild relative of the potato. In the late 1860s this insect switched its host food plant. By taking advantage of the widespread cultivation of potatoes, within 25 years it spread its range over the entire southwestern United States. We can say that the Colorado potato beetle was preadapted to feeding on potato plants by its resistance to the poisons in the leaves. Without such resistance it never could have exploited the potato farmers. Some scientists object to the word "preadaptation" because they feel it implies some sort of mystical forethought or purpose. But preadaptation is a useful concept when used to mean that some adaptation of the organism to its *present* environment is also useful in exploiting a *new* environment.

Animals in Transition?

Many animals today appear to be in the process of changing their basic way of life. Sea cucumbers generally live a quiet life in the mud on the sea bottom, but a few kinds have developed the ability to swim. While most jellyfish float with their mouths facing downward, one peculiar sort lies on its back in shallow water. Most birds fly, but flightless forms have evolved in several bird groups. In some the wings are useless, while penguins use their wings like powerful fins for swimming.

The most widespread and informative transition to study, however, is from aquatic to terrestrial living. The change from water-dwelling to land-living involves many drastic differences in habitat. While many organisms live successfully in the soil, representatives of only three major groups (phyla) of animals have been completely successful in colonizing land. All three were preadapted in important ways which enabled them successfully to invade land habitats.

Mollusks came equipped with a shell which protected them from drying out. Arthropods (insects, spiders, crabs, etc.) had a hard, external skeleton which helped support their weight on land and helped decrease water loss. Terrestrial vertebrates probably evolved from fish living in stagnant fresh-water swamps. These swamps dried up periodically. The fish which lived there were preadapted to life on land in several ways.

These fish were able to survive in stagnant water because they had a primitive lung capable of extracting oxygen from the air. They could survive drying out because they had tougher skin and perhaps special methods of conserving water. Their strong fins were adapted to movement along the bottom of the shallow swamps rather than to free swimming in open waters. All these traits helped them to colonize land.

Many animals of today appear to be in transition between life in the water and life on land. These organisms can survive at least for limited periods of time in either environment. But we cannot say what the future holds for them. We do not know if they are "on the way" to a terrestrial existence. The chances are, in fact, that they are not really evolving away from an aquatic existence. A species cannot take over a niche that is already occupied by another unless it is in some way better adapted to that niche. Since present land animals have been evolving for millions of years, they have become about as well adapted to land living as possible; a newcomer which is still struggling to "fit in" is not likely to displace them.

However, these organisms which live between two worlds are filling a niche themselves, one which enables them to take advantage of some characteristics of both water and land life. And it is always possible that in the future, new selection pressures will be placed on such flexible species, directing their evolution toward an increasingly terrestrial existence. By studying them, we can better understand something of the problems that go with terrestrial life.

A Fish Out of Water

At first it may seem surprising that many species of present-day fish frequently leave the water on purpose. But on second thought it seems less strange. Fish enemies live in water, and some fish are quite adept at leaving the water quickly to escape them. Small minnows will jump up in the air to avoid predators. This tactic is carried a bit further by a small fish of shallow water, the starhead topminnow, which actually flops out on land if it is pursued by an enemy. It lies on the shore for a while before jumping back in and is able to remember which direction to jump in to return.

Quite a few fish are able to travel fair distances through air to escape enemies. Needlefish take one leap after another, while garfish skim along the surface, using their tails as propellers. Flying fish are famous for their ability to leave the water. With favorable winds, these sea fish soar ten or even 20 feet above the water for as long as a minute. Whether or not any of these fish are evolving toward greater and greater ability to survive out of water is something scientists cannot say. But given the selection pressure provided by predators, the chances are that further refinements for survival out of water are being selected for.

Many fish which live in ponds or swamps can move over land when their homes are in danger of drying up, or per-

Flying fish can glide through the air for as long as a minute at present and may be evolving toward still greater out-of-water abilities.

haps when food becomes scarce. Long, thin fish like eels travel over land the same way they swim, with curves passing along their bodies. Snakeheads row with their fins while holding up their heads. These methods may seem awkward, but they get the fish from one body of water to another.

Some fish have special adaptations for overland travel. The climbing perch has strong, sharp spines on its gill covers. When "crawling," the fish spreads out the gill cover on one side, anchoring it firmly with the spine. Then it pushes forward with its strong fins and spreads the opposite gill cover for the next stroke. This fish is also able to use its gill cover spines to shinny up mangrove trees in search of insect prey. Like other fish out of water, it has a way of breathing in air. While many such fish have a lunglike swim bladder, the climbing perch has special air chambers near its gills.

One very successful fish which is able to travel on land is the walking catfish. A native of Thailand, this fish was brought to the United States by tropical-fish breeders for home aquariums. Like many other tropicals, the walking catfish were put in breeding ponds in warm southern Florida. The fish breeders were apparently unaware of the unique nature of this creature, and it wasn't long before many of their charges had hauled themselves out of the breeding ponds and flopped their way over land into the wild. As so often happens with introduced species, free from the natural enemies of their native land, the walking catfish now thrives in southern Florida. It has replaced native fishes in many areas, often by the simple tactic of eating them up.

This fascinating creature has several adaptations for survival on land. It ordinarily leaves water only at night, when the air is moist and the drying sun is gone. It has

The walking catfish of Florida and Thailand has become some-thing of a pest by its ability to travel over land. It cannot sur-vive cool weather at present, so its possible further spread is uncertain, depending on what additional evolutionary changes occur in this fish, or on possible climate changes, or both.

Mudskippers can spend as much as 90 per cent of their time out of water; some of them can even climb trees.

spines on its lower fins which can dig into the ground to help it move forward. Using its tail as well, it can travel as fast as five feet per minute over wet ground and may creep as far as a quarter mile over land between ponds. The walking catfish can obtain oxygen from the water or air; the rear portion of each gill has been modified into a lunglike organ.

In the late 1960s, the walking catfish alarmed many people with its rapid spread through the southern part of Florida. They were afraid this fish would take over the waters of much of the South within a few years, displacing the desirable native fish such as the largemouth bass. But fortunately the walking catfish cannot stand much cold and probably cannot survive temperatures below 7°C. (45°F.). This vulnerability should restrict its range to only the warmest southern part of Florida, unless it evolves a way of tolerating lower temperatures.

Of all the living fish which can travel on land, only the mudskippers are truly amphibious. Sometimes called walking gobies, these fish are found along the tropical shores of the Indian and western Pacific oceans and along the coast of tropical West Africa. Mudskippers may spend 90 per cent of their time out of water, feeding on insects, worms, small crabs, and snails. They live along mud flats and mangrove swamps. Some species can even climb quite well, using a pair of lower fins furnished with suction cups typical of gobies. These fins, used by tide pool gobies to cling to rocks, can be considered as a preadaptation for climbing in those mudskippers which have them.

Unlike some air-breathing fish, mudskippers can remain completely submerged without drowning. But they are also highly adapted to air-breathing. They fill their gills with a mixture of air and water, which helps keep the gills from drying out. Their skin is used for breathing, too, an adaptation to land life also found in frogs and salamanders.

As might be expected, mudskippers are quite agile on land. They hop along using their powerful tails and strong lower fins. The eyes bulge out at the top of the head from special sockets which contain water at the bottom. The fish can roll its eyes downward into these reservoirs to moisten them. With its adaptations for land and water life, the mudskipper is able to live on the tropical mud flats at low tide when the water is gone or at the highest tides when the mud flats are completely covered. Since it is now able to enjoy the best of both worlds, the likelihood is that these very successful creatures will continue to thrive.

Land Crabs and Their Kin

One of the most varied groups of animals found on to-day's earth is the crustaceans. Most people are familiar with shrimp, crabs, and crayfish but don't realize they're related to the different-looking beach hoppers and pill bugs. There are even crabs that climb trees. Several kinds of crustaceans have taken at least some evolutionary steps towards terrestrial life. And since they have been on land for less time than insects and vertebrates, they may still be in the process of refining their adaptations to life on land.

Until recently, no terrestrial shrimp was known. But in the late 1960s one was discovered along the Central and South American coast. This interesting animal shows only slight adaptations for life on land. Its legs are stronger than those of aquatic shrimps, which helps to support its weight on land. It lives among driftwood above the high-tide mark, hiding under the wood during the day and climbing out onto the logs at night. The success of this unique animal probably depends on its ability to escape predators. The nearby water, which it avoids, abounds in predators, and the ground underneath its driftwood home is frequented by hungry land crabs. Should some creature attempt to catch one of these shrimp up on the wood, it can escape by using its great talent, leaping. While less than an inch long, it can leap six inches high and cover a foot in one jump.

Other crustaceans have been evolving terrestrial adaptations for more generations and are better equipped for life

This close-up shows Merguia rhizophoreae, *a shrimp actually less than one inch long, that is adapting to life on land. It climbs on driftwood and mangrove roots at night, hiding under driftwood during the day.*

on land. The most familiar are the terrestrial isopods, often called wood lice, pill bugs, or sow bugs. The stunt of rolling up into a ball, which gives the pill bug its name, not only protects it from enemies but also helps it conserve water in dry conditions.

Terrestrial isopods are found in just about all land habitats, including beaches, forests, and even deserts. However, they lack the protective waxy outer layer which spiders

The sow bug is a crustacean thoroughly at home on land, though it still needs a damp habitat under wood, leaves, or stones.

and insects have evolved. Pill bugs must therefore live in relatively damp, protected places such as under stones or wood, or in burrows, venturing out only at night. Their gills can extract oxygen from the air but always need a protective film of moisture. Some wood lice have a complex system of surface channels that collect water and transport it to the gills, while others can join their tail parts together into a tube for drawing dew or rain water up to moisten the gills.

Many kinds of crabs have become at least partially terrestrial. Fiddler crabs, hermit crabs, and shore crabs live along the edge of the sea. The mangrove crab climbs mangrove trees and gnaws on their leaves. The coconut crab, which may weigh as much as 20 pounds, climbs up palm trees to feed on the fruits, husking them with its powerful claws.

While the different terrestrial crabs vary in their ability to live away from water, all must return to the sea to spawn. The females of some species carry the eggs around for awhile, but the larvae of all must develop in the water. Thus, none have become completely independent of the sea.

Back to the Water

We have just seen how some aquatic animals have become adapted to life out of water. Now we will look at a few land creatures which take advantage of the protection or food resources—or both—which water can provide.

Over the millions of years of evolution, selection pressures have acted on some groups of animals to become first adapted to land life and later to return to the water. Whales, porpoises, sea otters, and sea cows are mammals which

Other crustaceans have also adapted to land life, such as the coconut crab, above, and the mangrove crab, below.

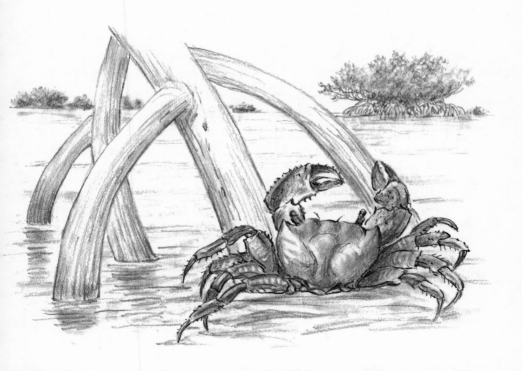

evolved gradually from terrestrial ancestors into superb examples of sleek aquatic beings.

The name "amphibian" means "both lives"—amphibians are generally animals which live both in water and on land. Most amphibians do need water to breed, but there are live-bearers which never return to water and egg-layers which also reproduce totally on land. Other amphibians, such as the mud puppy and the Surinam toad, live totally in the water and never venture out onto soil. The differing selection pressures of their varied habitats have molded them for different lives.

The ability to lay large eggs with a hard, protective shell freed reptiles from the need to return to water to reproduce. They have evolved water-resistant scales and other effective adaptations for land, so that reptiles are found even in the driest deserts. But among reptiles we nevertheless find some which have evolved at least somewhat to a watery life.

Many kinds of turtles have evolved toward an amphibious or aquatic life. Fresh-water pond turtles may be found by the shore or in the water. Their feet have become flattened and webbed, which makes for better swimming. The legs of sea turtles have evolved into flippers, for these reptiles return to land only to lay eggs. It is a slow process for the female sea turtle to haul herself up onto the beach to deposit these. Sea snakes are the most aquatic of reptiles. Their tails are flattened and rudder-like, and they can remain under water for two hours without returning to the surface. Some species must leave the water to lay eggs, but others are live-bearers and spend their entire lives in water, requiring only an occasional gulp of air for survival.

Other reptiles have taken only first, tentative steps

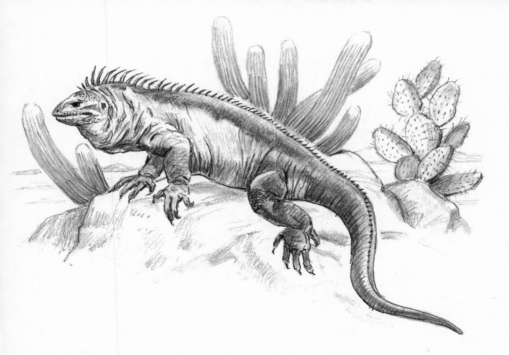

The land iguana, above, of the Galápagos Islands remains a complete land-dweller, but the marine iguana, below, can survive for long periods under the water.

toward an aquatic life. The green iguana often lives near the water. Female iguanas will swim to offshore islands to lay their eggs, and the young iguanas swim back to the mainland soon after hatching. Probably this pattern of reproduction evolved in response to heavy predator pressure on the mainland. These iguanas also take advantage of their comfort in the water by diving in like frogs when disturbed. They can stay under water for several minutes while the danger passes.

Perhaps the most interesting amphibious reptile is the famous marine iguana of the Galápagos Islands. The plants and animals of islands hold a special fascination for the student of evolution, for islands are "natural laboratories" of evolution. Initially populated by a few stray individuals from nearby continents, islands provide a whole new set of uninhabited niches into which the colonizing organisms can radiate. Darwin was much impressed by the diversity of obviously closely related species, especially birds, which he found on the Galápagos Islands. They provided persuasive evidence for the fact of evolution as a force operating not only in the past but in the present and future as well.

These islands are populated by both land and marine iguanas. While the land iguanas have kept their usual reptilian habitat, marine iguanas have evolved quite far toward aquatic life. They spend a great deal of time basking on rocks by the shore, to be sure, but they can survive under water for considerable periods of time, feeding on marine

The European and Asiatic water spider builds itself a "diving bell" with its silk, under which it keeps air trapped. Thus its evolution to underwater life has been relatively simple, not needing a gill-like system.

plants along the bottom. Their tails have become flattened like rudders and their toes are slightly webbed. Whether or not they are evolving further toward an aquatic existence is problematical. There appears to be greater danger from predators in the water than out. The iguanas seem to avoid water at high tide when sharks abound. If disturbed, they prefer hiding under a rock to diving in the sea.

The evolutionary path back to water has also been traced by certain insects. Some water bugs are quite well adapted to pond life with their oarlike legs, and water striders skimming along the surface are a familiar sight. The larvae of many insects such as dragonflies, mosquitoes, stone-flies, and mayflies also live in the water and have a variety of adaptations for aquatic living.

But perhaps one of the most interesting pond creatures is the one spider, found in Europe and Asia, which has successfully taken on an aquatic existence. This unusual creature carries air bubbles down to its underwater web. Here the bubbles become trapped by the silk, forming a natural "diving bell." The bell is the spider's home to which it returns to feed, mate, and lay eggs. By evolving a way to transfer the air it needs under water, this spider has found a way to live aquatically with only a few evolutionary changes.

5

The Minute World:
Molecules, Viruses, Bacteria

Our understanding of the genetic mechanisms which under-
lie all the phenomena of life has increased incredibly in the
last 20 years or so. We now know the chemical nature of
genes, and we have some understanding of how they determine the traits of organisms. This knowledge has pro-
found effects on theories of evolution and on the study of
its mechanisms and effects.

A class of chemicals called nucleic acids play the key
roles in genetic structure and function. The "star" is de-
oxyribonucleic acid, the famous DNA (with RNA as a
"supporting player" that we need not discuss in this book).
Genes consist simply of long molecules of DNA. But how
can such molecules contain the information which leads
ultimately to brown eyes or curly hair? The secret lies in
the unique chemical structure of the nucleic acids.

The DNA molecule is a polymer; that is, a chain of
smaller molecules bound together by chemical means into
a large one. The DNA "backbone" consists of a string of
identical molecules of a sugar called deoxyribose linked
together through phosphate molecules. Attached to one side
of each sugar molecule is another kind of chemical subunit.

Unlike the sugar molecules, these subunits are not identical. There are four subunits, named adenine, guanine, cytosine, and thymine. They are commonly abbreviated as A, G, C, and T.

The four subunits of the DNA molecule can be arranged in any order along the sugar backbone and are the key to understanding how DNA specifies the traits of an organism. The sequence of subunits is unique for each allele of each gene. This sequence is a code which contains the information for determining the trait governed by the gene.

The Vital Proteins

But now we are faced with the question, *How* does the unique sequence code for a certain trait? The answer is that the DNA sequence of subunits directs the making of particular protein molecules. Although we do not understand all the biochemical steps leading to the expression of most genetic traits, we do know that the key to the first step is usually a class of proteins called enzymes. These regulate the reactions of chemicals within the bodies of living things. Other kinds of proteins serve vital functions as well. Many important body parts, such as muscle and hair, are composed of certain proteins. (The actual shaping of embryos' developing bodies and organs depends also on such things as electrical and chemical communication between cells, move-

The double helix of DNA, above. The diagram below shows a DNA molecule replicating, or copying itself; the original spiral separates and the necessary subunits move into the empty spaces, chemically "locking themselves" in place with the participation of the proper enzymes.

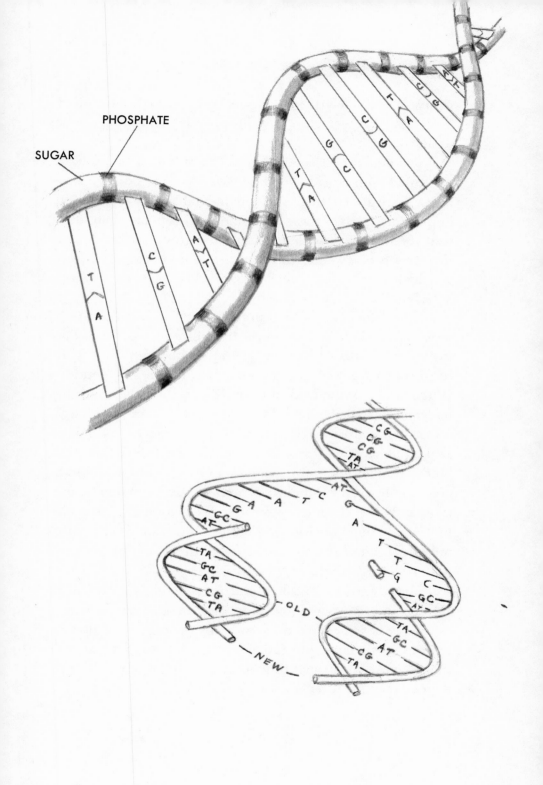

PHOSPHATE

SUGAR

ments of cells, relative timing of tissue growth, and other processes. These factors are just barely beginning to be understood.)

Proteins are also polymers. The subunits of proteins are called amino acids. While DNA has four possible subunits, there are 20 different fundamental amino acids found in proteins. Each of these 20 amino acids consists of an identical chemical unit with a unique side group attached. The side group of glycine, the simplest amino acid, is merely one hydrogen atom. Other amino acids, such as tyrosine, have large, complex side groups.

The backbone of the amino acid chain consists of a series of the identical chemical units linked together. The side groups project away from the backbone. A molecule consisting of a few amino acids is called a polypeptide. When many amino acids are linked together, the resulting molecule is called a protein. Proteins are often very large molecules, consisting of long chains of hundreds of amino acids. But each of these is always one of the fundamental 20 kinds. Many other amino acids do exist—hundreds of kinds are found serving other functions in living systems, and thousands are chemically possible. Although a few modifications of them occasionally occur after proteins are built, only the fundamental 20 amino acids are found in the proteins of living things.

Because of chemical interactions among the different side groups, protein molecules take on particular shapes once they have been manufactured by the cell. They do not exist as long chains, but rather become folded up into complex shapes. The proper functioning of the protein molecule depends on this three-dimensional shape.

The DNA Code

The four subunits of the DNA molecule determine the sequence of the twenty possible amino acids through a simple code. Each of the DNA subunits is like a "letter" in a word, and each "word" of the DNA code has three "letters." If you try to arrange the four letters A, G, C, and T in all possible three-letter combinations—AAA, AAG, AGT, ACG, TGC, GGC, and so forth—you will see that there are 64 possible combinations. Thus the DNA code has 64 possible words, more than enough to code for, or "give orders" for, the 20 amino acid subunits we find in proteins. Using sophisticated experiments and patient, hard work, scientists have been able to unravel the DNA code. They know which DNA word codes for which amino acid. For example, the sequence ACA codes for an amino acid called cystine; GAA codes for an amino acid named leucine. They also know that some amino acids are determined by more than one DNA word; for example, AGA, AGG, TCA, and TCG all code for the amino acid serine. They also know that three words are nonsense words. These nonsense words act as periods, signifying the end of the instructions for the structure of a given protein molecule.

The details of how the DNA information for protein structure is translated by the cell can be found elsewhere and are not necessary for understanding the impact of the new knowledge about DNA on evolutionary biology. It is important, however, to keep in mind a few facts about the DNA code. The code is continuous along the DNA and is "read" in groups of three subunits. For example, the sequence ACATCGGAATCG would be translated by the cell into the production of a protein molecule with the structure *cystine-serine-leucine-serine*. Because some amino acids are coded by more than one DNA word, more than one DNA sequence can result in the same amino acid sequence. For example, ACATCAGAAAGG would also lead to the manufacture of the above amino acid sequence.

Just how DNA is organized into chromosomes is not yet understood. But we do know how the DNA sequence is copied so that each cell contains the same genetic information.

The DNA of a gene does not exist as a single-stranded molecule. Rather, it consists of two long strands which are wound around each other, forming a spiral called a double helix. The sugar backbones of the strands are around the outside of the helix while the subunits containing the code project towards the inside. The double helix is a stable chemical structure because the subunits are bound to one another across the helix by weak chemical bonds. But because of their size and shape, the subunits can bind only in certain combinations. A always binds to T and G always binds to C. Therefore, if one knows the sequence of one strand of a DNA molecule, one can predict the sequence of its complementary strand. For example, the sequence ATCCGTA would be paired with the sequence TAGG-CAT. This vital fact about DNA chemistry is what makes the genetic continuity between cells of an organism possible and enables the organisms of one generation to pass their traits on to their offspring.

Identical Twins of DNA

Before a cell divides, it manufactures a new set of identical DNA. Thus the cell before division contains two identical sets of genetic instructions. During the synthesis of the new DNA, the double helix of the DNA molecule is unwound and the two strands separate. A new complementary strand is then produced along each half of the old DNA molecule. Since the sequence of subunits on each strand determines the sequence of its complementary strand, the two double helixes which result are both identical to the original one. Each new helix consists of one old DNA strand paired with one new strand. When all the old DNA has been copied in this way, the cell contains two identical copies of all the genes of all the chromosomes. Thus, when the cell divides, each "daughter" cell receives an identical set of genetic instructions.

The Chemistry of Mutation

Although the DNA copying mechanism of the cell is extremely accurate, occasionally it makes mistakes. They are caused by such things as certain chemicals, ion radiation, ultraviolet, even heat sometimes. These mistakes result in the mutations upon which evolution acts. Now that we know the molecular basis of heredity, we can understand why some mutations result in trivial changes while others result in drastic changes.

The most common sort of mutation is a subunit substitution; the wrong subunit is inserted into the new DNA strand during its duplication (generally called replication in genetic discussion). The effects of this sort of mutation depend on many things. A trivial change which has no effect on the phenotype would result, for example, from a mutation from AGA to AGG, since both of these triplets code for the same amino acid, serine. However, a drastic change might result from a mutation to a nonsense triplet. In that case, only part of the protein molecules would be manufactured, since the nonsense triplet codes for a stop. If this mutation occurred near the beginning of the gene, only a small piece of the protein would be formed. If it occurred near the end, most of the protein would be formed. Thus the effect of a mutation to a nonsense word depends on where in the gene the mutation occurs. It also depends on how important the missing piece is to the folding of the protein molecule which gives it its shape.

Probably the most important sort of mutation is one resulting in an amino acid substitution within the protein coded for. For example, a mistake which substituted the triplet ACC for ACA would lead to a protein with the amino acid tryptophan instead of cystine in that position. As you will soon see, scientists debate the overall importance of these mutations to evolutionary change, but some of them have spectacular results.

A classic example is that of human hemoglobins. Hemoglobin is a vital protein found in the red blood cells. Its molecules bind with oxygen as blood circulates through the capillaries in the lungs and carry the oxygen to cells in all parts of the body. Normal hemoglobin molecules are bound together in a certain way within the red blood cells. Abnormal forms of hemoglobin are also found in humans. The most famous of these is hemoglobin S, which is linked to the sickle-cell trait. This differs from the normal hemoglobin A by a single amino acid.

This one small change results in drastic effects for the person homozygous for hemoglobin S. The one amino acid difference in the protein results in a change in the shape of the hemoglobin molecules so that they do not form a stable disk-shaped red blood cell. Instead, when little oxygen is present in the blood, the red blood cells collapse into sickle-shaped cells, which clog the minute blood capillaries, resulting in great pain and in serious symptoms such as anemia, brain damage, and kidney failure.

Another defective human hemoglobin, hemoglobin C, also differs from the normal molecule in the same amino acid. The effects of hemoglobin C are not as severe as those of hemoglobin S, but it does cause anemia. The reasons for the high frequency of these two alleles in certain human populations, despite their bad effects, will be explored later.

Viruses—Evolution in Action

Are viruses alive? This question has been debated over and over again by scientists, and no agreement has been reached. Part of the trouble lies in finding a satisfactory definition of "alive." After learning something of these fascinating little particles, you can try to make up your own mind.

A virus is an amazingly simple object. It consists of a piece of nucleic acid wrapped up in a protein coat. The simplest viruses have only these two constituents; some of them also contain a very few other components. Outside a living cell the virus is inert and metabolically inactive. But once it has infected a cell, the virus literally takes over. The viral nucleic acid directs the cell to produce virus particles. The cell becomes merely a virus "factory," making more and more virus particles. These particles then infect other cells and cause production of still more viruses. When the level of infection becomes high enough, the infected organism will show the symptoms of the viral disease. The common cold and influenza are the most familiar viral

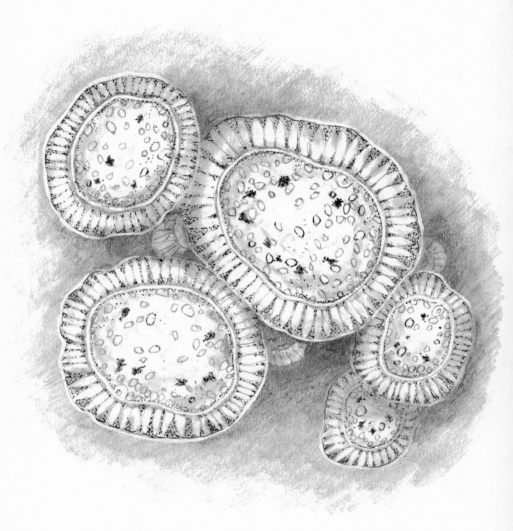

Viruses of Hong Kong flu, magnified well over 300,000 times. Within them are proteins and pieces of RNA (an information-code chemical rather similar to DNA). The centers are surrounded by double fatty layers; infection begins when the spiky protein projections attach the viruses to host cells.

diseases that our human race is afflicted by.

Viruses provide fine examples of evolution in action. The constant evolutionary changes of viruses keep thousands of public health workers busy all over the world. It is impossible to immunize people against the common cold because it is brought about by a great variety of viruses. Every year new strains of influenza appear—the Hong Kong flu, Victoria flu, swine flu, and others. Public health workers are in a constant race with these new strains, trying to develop vaccines effective against each one before another strain emerges.

The evolution of viruses follows the same course as evolution in plants and animals. A new virus comes along. Host organisms are susceptible to it because the outer protein coat is different from that of previous viral strains and the host's immune system cannot attack it. For a while this strain is very successful, until it has infected many members of the host population and they have become immune to it. Now selection will favor a new viral strain different enough from the last one to infect the population all over again. Because of the huge number of virus particles produced during infection, the chances of mutants with a somewhat different protein coat being produced are very high. These mutants will be selected for and will go on successfully to infect host organisms which are immune to the previous strain. This process can go on and on.

The influenza viruses are especially powerful infectors. They are constantly changing and evolving into new types. Their remarkable evolutionary success is due to two factors. Since they infect the respiratory passages, they are out of reach of some of the body's best defenses. They can multiply to some extent even in an immune host. And large numbers mean a greater chance of mutations to new, perhaps sufficiently different forms.

In addition, the nucleic acid of the influenza virus is in several pieces rather than one long strand. If two or more influenza viruses of different strains infect the same cell, their genetic information will be combined in some of the resulting virus particles, leading to even greater variability. Scientists have found that influenza viruses of distant strains, such as those infecting horses and those of humans, can recombine genetically. These scientists even suggest that perhaps *all* influenza viruses of the entire animal kingdom make up a common gene pool, leading to an infinite variety of different possible viruses of this disease.

Bacteria Everywhere

Bacteria are very small, single-celled organisms found in every possible habitat on earth. The word "bacteria" usually brings to mind "germs" and sickness. But most bacteria are harmless, and many kinds are very helpful. For example, our intestines teem with helpful bacteria which aid in the proper digestion of food. If one takes antibiotics for an infection and suffers the side effects of an upset stomach, it is because the antibiotic has killed off the helpful bacteria along with the harmful ones.

Bacteria are so plentiful that each human body carries around more of them than there are humans on this earth. They are the smallest organisms able to metabolize and reproduce independently. Their structure is simpler than that of plant and animal cells; they are no longer considered plants, as they once were, but are classified separately as Monera, along with the blue-green algae. The "nucleus"

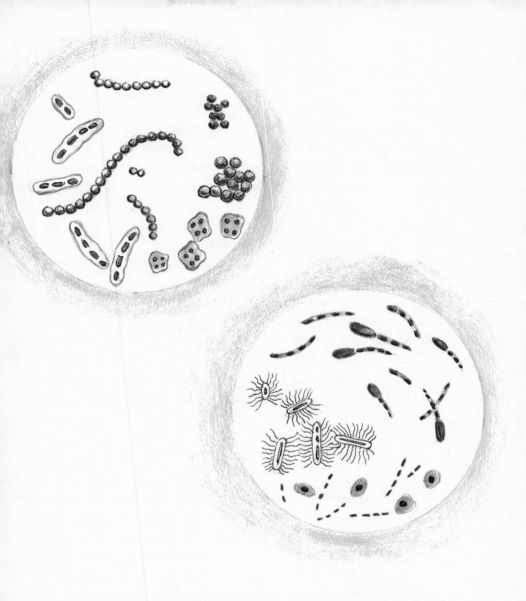

Above, cocci, or ball-shaped bacteria. Among the diseases caused by cocci are streptococcus infections (as in "strep throat"), lobar pneumonia, meningitis, boils, and septicemia ("blood poisoning"). Below are rod-shaped bacteria, called bacilli; among the diseases bacilli cause are diphtheria, typhoid fever, dysentery, whooping cough, and tuberculosis. Some bacteria have spiral and other shapes.

of the bacterial cell is simply a single continuous circle of double-stranded DNA. It is wound up inside the cell and is about 1000 times as long as the bacterium itself. The bacterial cell ordinarily contains only one allele of each gene instead of two. There is no nuclear membrane, and cell division is simpler than in higher organisms. Male and female sexes do not exist in bacteria, but they do have ways of exchanging genetic information.

Bacterial cultures are ideal for the study of evolution. Bacteria in culture can divide as often as every 20 minutes, giving an extremely short generation time. The mutation rate of specific genes varies from one in 100,000 to one in 16 billion cells per generation. Since one culture tube contains millions of bacterial cells, a large population exists in which appropriate mutations have a good chance of arising. And the conditions of culture can result in very strong selection pressures.

Bacteria and Medicine

Understanding the principles of evolution and using them to human advantage is very important in medicine when dealing with microorganisms. A common technique in medical laboratories is to take a virulent strain of bacteria and grow it in culture. At first it grows slowly. But with repeated transfers to fresh growth media, the culture improves in growth. Through the continual natural selection of mutant cells adapted to growth on the medium the bacterial population becomes better and better adapted to life in the laboratory.

Meanwhile, however, those cells best adapted to life in a host organism are being selected against. Thus laboratory culture often results in a decreased virulence of the disease organism. This is called attenuation. This method is widely used in obtaining weakened strains of both bacteria and viruses for use in vaccines. And if a more virulent strain is desired again, this can be accomplished by inoculating an animal with a large number of bacterial cells. In the animal's body, selection pressures will now favor the multiplication of the mutants which are best able to grow inside an animal host.

Knowledge of evolution is also important in the treatment of bacterial disease, for some bacteria frequently produce drug-resistant mutants. These resistant strains are of two types. Each requires a different kind of treatment. Certain drug-resistant strains tend to arise through an accumulation of mutations, each of which adds a bit more resistance. The diseases they produce are best treated by giving the patient a large enough dose of the drug to kill off the disease organisms fast, before chance allows a first-step mutant to arise.

Other forms of drug resistance originate from a one-step mutation to a high level of resistance. These infections are treated by giving two different antibiotics at once. The chance of a bacterial cell's developing the two mutations necessary for resistance to both drugs is very small. For example, if the chance of mutation to resistance to one drug is one in a million, and of mutation to resistance to the other drug is one in 10 million, then the chance of a double mutant, resistant to both drugs, is one in ten trillion.

6
Monkey Wrenches:
Interference by Humans

Antibiotics have been invaluable tools in treating bacterial diseases. But their use has led to serious problems as well.

In 1959 antibiotics were being used in Japan to treat an outbreak of a severe form of dysentery caused by a bacterium called Shigella. Doctors became alarmed when strains of Shigella appeared which were resistant to all four antibiotics used in treatment of the disease. It seemed impossible that one strain could acquire all the necessary chance mutations so rapidly, if at all. Studies showed that other species of intestinal bacteria shared the resistance, and that the multiple drug resistance could be transferred as a package from one bacterium to another, even if the two were of different species.

We now know that the genes for drug resistance are passed from cell to cell by tiny circles of extrachromosomal genetic material called R factors. They can be transferred by a bacterial mating process (conjugation) to just about all species of intestinal bacteria, helpful and harmful alike. Resistance to at least ten different antibiotics can be transferred by R factors. Although no one factor known has all ten genes, new resistance genes can be added to the repertoire of existing R factors in nature and passed on to other bacteria.

The spread of R factors is ominous. In 1954 only 0.2 per cent of Shigella isolated from patients in Japan had multiple drug resistance. But by 1964, 52 per cent were resistant. In 1965 a survey of Japanese patients showed that 50 per cent of all intestinal bacteria carried R factors, while 65 per cent of dysentery-causing organisms had them. The seriousness of this situation was brought home in a recent epidemic of Shigella in Central America. The drug-resistant strain causing the outbreak killed 20 per cent of the infected children.

Once formed, a suitable R factor can spread very rapidly because of the extreme selection pressure of drug therapy. This situation leaves doctors with a serious di-lemma. They must be sparing in their use of antibiotic therapy to avoid increasing selection for drug resistance. Whether to treat mild cases of bacterial dysentery with drugs and risk the emergence of strains with multiple re-sistance or to let the patients suffer through the painful course of the disease is not an easy decision to make. Very ill or very young patients must be given antibiotics, but first the epidemic strain of bacteria has to be tested to see which drugs will eliminate it.

Disease treatment is not the only cause of the increase in bacterial drug resistance. It is routine practice to add antibiotics to the food of domestic animals and of fish in fisheries. There is good evidence that this practice helps human intestinal bacteria develop resistance to the anti-biotics. In Great Britain some attention has been paid to the spread of drug-resistant bacteria. There, antibiotics used for the treatment of human diseases are not allowed to be added to cattle feed. Such laws provide at least a beginning in dealing with the unpleasant consequences of this striking example of evolution in action.

Fortunately for us, not all kinds of infectious bacteria evolve drug resistance easily. While such resistance in organisms causing dysentery, tuberculosis, and staphylococcus infections is clinically very important, many other bacteria rarely become resistant. We do not understand just why the genetic makeup of some species is prone to such mutations while others are not. The dangerous bacterium Streptococcus, which causes strep throat, scarlet fever, and rheumatic fever, can still be treated effectively with penicillin, the first antibiotic developed. Even in the laboratory it is very hard to obtain penicillin-resistant strains of Streptococcus, and those which do show up lack virulence.

Pesticide Resistance

One of the most important lessons to be learned from the controversy over chemical pesticide use is the power of natural selection. When DDT use began in the early 1940s, hopes were high that we had found the ideal way to vanquish our insect enemies. It wasn't long, however, before the bubble burst. In 1946 reports of houseflies resistant to DDT began coming in. By 1948 resistance was reported in 12 insect species, and by 1966 more than 165 species had resistant populations. When used on a pest population, DDT acts as a powerful selective agent, favoring the survival and reproduction of any resistant mutants. Use of other pesticides results in the same dilemma; by using the chemical killer, we increase the likelihood of a resistant population's emerging.

The ways of pesticide resistance are varied; any mutation which gives a selective advantage in the face of a poisonous assault is favored. Somtimes a change in the insects'
behavior results in less exposure to the poison. In other cases,
the outer cuticle of the insect becomes resistant to absorb-
ing pesticides, so less enters the body. But the most effective
forms of resistance are quite specific, such as the formation
of enzymes which break down the pesticide molecules, making them harmless. Ordinarily such forms of resistance are
limited to the particular pesticide used. But sometimes they
are more general. For example, a strain of body lice which
developed DDT resistance was also resistant to another
class of insecticides called pyrethrins, but not to Malathion.

Resistance to DDT arises so consistently that it has been
possible to study the course of events in some detail. In
housefly and mosquito populations, DDT resistance usually
develops within two years of exposure to the chemical. It
commonly proceeds in two steps. First, a single mutation to
a partially dominant allele for resistance arises and spreads
rapidly. This is followed by a rapid increase in resistance
caused by further mutations of modifying genes which step
up the action of the original mutation.

At this point we might ask ourselves if perhaps exposure to pesticides stimulates resistance in some non-
random way. An interesting experiment carried out on
fruit flies shows that this does not happen—at least with the
species tested. In this investigation, scientists raised families
of fruit flies separately. From each family, some of the
brother and sister flies were exposed to DDT while others
were not. If the individuals from a certain family showed
resistance, the unexposed flies from that family were bred
and tested for DDT resistance. The experiment was carried

on for several generations and resistance was increased, despite the fact that none of the flies which were bred were ever exposed to the chemical; only their relatives were.

These results show that resistant mutants occur naturally in populations whether or not they are exposed to insecticides. Ordinarily, such resistant individuals suffer some disadvantages compared to normal nonmutants and are actually selected against. But such a powerful selective agent as a deadly poison immediatly reverses the direction of selection, leaving an open field for any resistant strains which can survive.

Now that we know we cannot solely rely on insecticides to control insect pests, scientists are finding alternative ways of controlling them. Other considerations aside, such as the killing of highly beneficial insects like bees and the accumulation of possibly dangerous chemicals in the environment, poisons just are not adquate as a means of pest control. Statistics are on the side of the insect—the large populations, short generation times, and high reproductive potentials of pest species all favor the eventual selection of resistant mutants. Poisons are also used against other pests such as rats, but longer generation times and smaller populations have kept the number of resistant populations to a minimum so far.

Evolution and Pollution

Among the many effects civilization has had on the earth is pollution. This takes many forms, and its effects on the living world are usually too gradual and subtle to assess. A few dramatic examples, such as the industrial melanism in moths we took up earlier, have been intensively studied.

Garbage thrown from fish trawlers has enabled the fulmar petrels to extend their range a good deal.

Other effects, such as the extinction of some species and the increase in population of others, have not been as thoroughly investigated.

One good example of human effects on natural populations is the spread of a bird called the fulmar petrel. This sea bird used to breed on only one island in the British Isles off Scotland. But since the last quarter of the nineteenth century it has increased its range to include sites on many Scottish inland sites as well as along the Scottish mainland, Ireland, Wales, and parts of England.

This dramatic spread of the fulmar's range is due to changes in the amount and distribution of its food. While the fulmar ordinarily feeds mainly on microscopic sea life, it will eat also the remains of dead animals. In the nineteenth century the northern fisheries of Great Britain were concerned with whaling, and the fulmar petrel would eat the remains of the whale carcasses from the water. But when whaling declined, ice-carrying fish trawlers took the place of whaling ships. The fish are cleaned on board the ships, and vast quantities of fish organs are thrown overboard, providing plenty of food for the fulmar petrel over its expanded range.

The practices of human beings have, however, reduced the range of other birds, bringing them to the verge of extinction. Sometimes even when we try to help nature, we make mistakes. The Kirtland's warbler of Michigan requires young jack pines for nesting sites. But periodic forest fires are necessary to stimulate the release of seeds by jack pine cones and to make space for the young trees. Our efforts to suppress forest fires reduced the habitat of this bird and therefore reduced its population to a dangerously low level. Fortunately, foresters have learned more about the natural role of fire in the cycle of the forest and have been allowing selected fires to burn under careful control, providing habitats for species such as the jack pine and Kirtland's warbler again.

Kirtland's warbler needs jack pine trees, and the trees need periodic forest fires to do well. Natural fires set by lightning are now allowed to burn sufficiently to insure the birds' survival.

Rabbits and Viruses

Sometimes coevolution can proceed fast enough for scientists to document it, especially when we have interfered with nature. The effects can be dramatic. The European rabbit was introduced into Australia by humans. With no natural enemies but with plenty of grass to eat, rabbits multiplied at an alarming rate. They became a plague, endangering agriculture and native wildlife.

Scientists trying to find a way to control the rabbits found a virus, called myxomatosis, which caused a mild disease in South American rabbits. European rabbits, however, were killed by it. When the virus was introduced into Australia it was startlingly effective. Within six weeks a sample population dropped from 5000 to 50. Mortality was 99.8 per cent.

People thought that the rabbit problem was solved. But it wasn't long before more and more rabbits were surviving the disease. Today, although the rabbit population is nowhere near the former plague levels, there are more than enough rabbits in Australia.

What happened? Two factors contributed to the rabbit's comeback. Selection favored any rabbits with some resistance to myxomatosis, so the animals became less susceptible. But even more important, natural selection acted on the virus. Myxomatosis in Australia is carried from one rabbit to another by mosquitoes. Virus strains which don't kill their hosts will infect more rabbits than strains which do kill, since mosquitoes bite only living animals. Thus the less virulent strain will come to predominate. Several times, deadly strains of myxomatosis have been reintroduced into

Australia. Each time they have rapidly died out because they were selected against.

Resistant Grasses

One of the messiest of human activities is mining. Great quantities of rock and dirt are brought out and left in huge piles around the landscape. Since the dirt comes from deep underground where plants and animals do not live, it contains no fertilizing organic matter to nourish plants. A more serious problem is the frequently high content of poisonous heavy metals in such mine tailings and slag heaps. Ordinary plants cannot grow in the presence of high concentrations of heavy metals. Root growth is inhibited and the plants die.

Fortunately, natural selection again shows its power, and our understanding of it is leading to better solutions in dealing with the unsightly and often dangerous mounds of mine waste littering the countryside of mining districts.

Study of this problem has been especially intense in Great Britain. Several kinds of plants have been found growing on mine tailings. The most common are two kinds of grass. Scientists have studied the heavy-metal tolerance of different races of such plants and have found that populations from uncontaminated areas lack tolerance. Plants which can grow in soil with copper are tolerant of only copper; plants from soil containing copper and zinc are tolerant of both. Thus evolution is again doing its steady, quiet work and the specific tolerance required for living in a particular environment has been selected for.

Study of these resistant grasses has led to hopes for inexpensive and effective reclamation of mine tailings. In the

Festuca, a type of grass, has evolved so that it can live near mine smelters where there is a concentration of heavy metals, ordinarily poisonous, in the soil.

past, topsoil and fertilizer were spread over the mounds and
ordinary grasses seeded there. They grew for a while but
eventually died, probably because their roots reached the
poisonous heap below. But more recently, some heaps have
been treated with fertilizer alone and then seeded with
native tolerant grasses. The grass has thrived and has grown
as well as ordinary strains in normal pastures. Fortunately,
fertilizing and seeding with native tolerant strains costs only
one-sixth as much as covering the heaps with topsoil and
fertilizer and seeding with ordinary grasses.

While the evolution of such tolerant plants probably
had a head start because of initial high levels of minerals in
the soil around mines, metal tolerance can evolve with
amazing rapidity in a very small area. In 1936 a fence made
of galvanized netting was put up at a particular location in
England. Galvanized wire is treated with zinc to protect it
from rusting. The fence was renewed in 1958. In the early
1960s a curious scientist tested plants growing at its foot.
He found that in fewer than 30 years, plants of two species
growing there were significantly tolerant of zinc compared
to normal plants a few feet away. Later laboratory studies
have shown that such tolerance may become fully established in only five generations.

7

Plants and Animals for Our Use

We humans have had our most spectacular impact on the evolution of living things by modifying them to meet our own needs. In the wild, natural selection tends to weed out mutations leading to dangerously unusual features. A white rabbit is very conspicious in the woods and would fall easy prey to an enemy. The teeth of a short-muzzled wolf would be crammed together in its misshapen jaw. That animal would have a difficult time killing prey and ripping off its share of the kill. But since many such characteristics are caused by recessive genes, they are present in natural populations, carried passively along in unaffected heterozygotes. When humans pick out a small number of wild individuals and breed them together at the beginnings of domestication, the resulting inbreeding rapidly brings out the effects of the hidden recessive alleles, and new phenotypes emerge. If these phenotypes are pleasing or useful, they will be preserved when humans choose those animals as breeding stock. This is called artificial selection, as opposed to the natural selection process which occurs in the wild.

Domestication can lead to very rapid evolutionary changes. As soon as a species is chosen for domestication and comes under human control, great shifts in selection pressures occur. Though such traits as protective coloration, wariness, and synchronized breeding are strongly selected for in the wild, their opposites may be valued by humans.

Many domesticated animals are bred for their pelts, and people enjoy a variety of fur colors. Minks have been domesticated for only about 40 years, but already there are over 100 coat-color variations in domesticated minks. Some of these are caused by the combination of several recessive mutations. Minks with long, angora-type fur are also bred. Most of these mutations have effects beyond the color and form of the fur. The majority, when present in homozygous form, cause also a decrease in fertility and vitality. In nature, these animals wouldn't last long. But in the protected environment we provide, they can reach maturity and reproduce.

Minks have been bred exclusively for their variations in coat. Despite the many generations of minks which have lived in captivity, people who handled these feisty animals have to wear heavy gloves for protection against bites. But other animals have become tame and unafraid, or even friendly, through domestication. Just like coat color, docility can be selected by humans. Russian workers have shown this by selecting, within 15 years, a strain of docile, tranquil foxes that approach the dog in behavior.

While selecting for nonwild behavior, these scientists may also have discovered why so many domesticated animals lose their natural reproductive rhythms. While most wild animals breed at only one time of year, many domesticated animals, such as dogs, will breed the year round. Behavior and reproduction are controlled in large part by the interaction of the brain and the hormones of the body. In the

Breeding under human supervision that takes full advantage of
mutations has produced more than a hundred coat-color variations in the domesticated mink, below. In its natural state the
mink does not change this characteristic so easily.

foxes selected for tranquil behavior, the reproductive rhythm is disturbed. These animals breed much earlier in the season and are more fertile than other foxes. Perhaps in selecting for behavior suitable for domestication, we have also selected for less precise breeding rhythms in our captives.

We can exert selection pressures in favor of whatever traits we wish in our domestic stock. We can do so either by selecting the specimens which most closely approach our goal or by capitalizing on a rare mutation. If we want big plants or animals, we can select the largest individuals for breeding. Over several generations, the average size of the specimens will increase. Or we may be lucky and have a natural giant appear in the stock, which can transmit the trait to offspring.

There are a good many examples of gradual artificial selection in a desired direction. Since 1900, strains of corn with high and low oil content have been selected, starting from the same ordinary field corn population. The oil content of the original strain varied from 3.9 to 6 per cent. By 1950 the strain selected for low oil content had about 1 per cent oil, while the high strain was up to 15 per cent. Such selection must eventually approach a limit. There will always be some oil present in the corn, and a maximum possible limit must also exist.

Sometimes we may want to select for two traits that cannot easily be selected together. If cattle are bred for increased milk production, the fat content of the milk decreases. This is a problem to breeders, for the most desirable milk has a high fat content. Through modern complex techniques of artificial selection, it is possible to partially overcome such difficulties. Modern milk cows give large amounts of milk with a fat content of nearly 5 per cent.

However, this is still less than half the 10 to 12 per cent of wild cattle ancestors.

Artificial selection of rare mutants has also been a useful tool of plant breeders. Some of our best varieties of cultivated plants have arisen as rare mutations. For example, the popular golden delicious apple originated as a single mutant tree in one orchard. Fortunately for apple-lovers, it was noticed and carefully nurtured. Useful mutations in domestic animals are very rare. With smaller populations and longer generation times than plants, domestic animal populations would be expected to yield few useful new mutations.

Plant Breeding—What For?

Depending on the uses to which they are put, plants are selected by us for many different kinds of traits. While commercial corn may be selected for heavy, simultaneous yield, corn for the home garden may be bred for a continuous yield of especially sweet ears. Tomatoes for mass production are bred for tough skins, firm flesh, and simultaneous ripening, characteristics necessary for mechanically harvested fruits. Home gardeners, on the other hand, want a continuous yield of tender, thin-skinned tomatoes. Vegetable varieties for the South must be able to withstand heat, while those for the North need to ripen as early as possible. Some flower varieties are grown for large, spectacular blossoms while others are selected for numerous, compact blooms.

Because the genetic material provided by nature does not always correspond with human desires, some varieties have taken many years to develop. In 1954 the Burpee Seed

Company announced that it would pay $10,000 to the first person who developed a pure white marigold with flowers at least two and a half inches across. Flower gardeners all over the country did their best to accomplish this goal. Burpee received 8208 seed samples. Testing these samples plus running their own research toward the white marigold cost the company over a quarter of a million dollars. Finally, in 1976, the search was over and, with great fanfare, a check for $10,000 was awarded to Mrs. Alice Vonk, an amateur gardener from Iowa. Although the white marigold is the most expensive flower ever developed in the world, others such as the black tulip have also been difficult to achieve.

Breeding Disease Resistance

Since insects consistently develop resistance to pesticides, the breeding of plant strains with resistance to pests and diseases has been receiving more and more attention recently. For a long time, emphasis in this field was on resistance to diseases, such as rusts, for which no chemical means of control had been developed.

As with selection for any other trait, breeding for disease resistance can be approached in two ways. The grower can select for gradual buildup of "horizontal resistance," which probably involves several different genes. Its characteristic is the accumulation of many small effects. Horizontal resistance is usually effective against more than one pest strain.

The other method yields "vertical resistance," which is usually due to a single dramatic effect on the pest or disease. In the past, the tendency has been to treat sample plants with heavy doses of the disease organism and select genotypes with unusual resistance. Although this method gives fast, impressive results, unfortunately it results in selection of very specific resistance. The new strain may not be resistant against all races of the disease. Such vertical resistance is also more easily overcome by natural selection of the pest organism. The war between the plant breeder and the pest can go on and on. In apples there are at least 19 different ways of initiating what is probably the same mechanism of resistance to scab fungus. Unfortunately, the fungus has evolved 19 corresponding ways to avoid tripping the resistance alarm.

From this one example it is easy to see why vertical resistance often fails after early success. As more and more acres are planted with the new, resistant strain, the selection pressure for new races of the pest is increased. And since only the one vertical-resistance mechanism has been selected for, genetic drift and founder effects have probably resulted in a *loss* of whatever horizontal resistance was previously present. As a result, once a pest mutant appears which can get around the resistance, the infestation is likely to be even worse than in an older variety with more generalized horizontal resistance.

Inbreeding and Genetic Variability

Inbreeding presents other problems besides the loss of valuable traits like horizontal disease resistance. Many damaging alleles are recessive and will show up in the homozygous state more frequently with inbreeding. Many of our dog breeds are plagued by a high frequency of bad traits caused by inbreeding. Malformation of the hips is common in German shepherds, while epilepsy often occurs in Labrador retrievers. Certain strains of Irish setters have an abnormal suspiciousness and hostility. A long list of such examples could easily be made.

Plant breeders have begun to recognize the importance of keeping a genetic diversity in cultivated plants. Wild relatives of domestic species, as well as old varieties successfully cultivated before modern agricultural techniques, are being used more and more often as sources for introducing genetic variability into inbred strains. There is even a plant-introduction center with regional offices which maintains a systematic collection of seeds from wild and old varieties. These seeds can be used by plant breeders in their experiments with developing new varieties.

Artificial Mutation

Another way to increase the genetic variability available for artificial selection is through artificial mutation. Exposure to X-rays, ultraviolet radiation, or certain chemicals can increase the mutation rate. This method has been used extensively in plant breeding to obtain new genotypes. New varieties of many flowers such as tulips, carnations, and snapdragons have been developed in this way. Crops such as barley, peanuts, oats, rice, and sugar beets have also been improved through creating mutations and then selecting. Improvement in the yield of antibiotics from the fungi which produce them has also been achieved through such methods, but its use in animals has been very limited. Because of the random, undirected nature of the increased mutation, very large numbers of individuals must be used to achieve any result. This is easy with plants and fungi, but not with domesticated animals.

Foster Mothers, Cloning, Cell Fusion

Recently acquired knowledge about basic biology is also being applied to the development of better plants and animals for our use. It is common practice now to transfer embryos of cattle across the ocean in the uterus of a female rabbit. After arriving at the destination, the embryos are removed from the rabbit and artificially implanted into "foster mother" cows. They grow there normally, and the cows give birth to healthy calves which are genetically unrelated to them.

Another technique which is being explored for its practical applications is called cloning. A clone is a group of genetically identical individuals. The parthenogenetic lizards mentioned earlier form natural clones, since the offspring are genetically identical to their mother. Artificial clones of carrots can be produced by modern techniques. Cells from a single carrot plant are separated and isolated. The individual cells can then be cultured. Each cell will divide and reproduce to form a complete carrot plant which is genetically identical to the other plants derived from the same original carrot. Cloning is being studied as a way of producing high-quality timber trees as well. Artificial selection of such wind-pollinated, slowly growing plants is difficult and time-consuming. But if clones could be grown from especially strong, healthy trees, whole forests of superior trees could be planted. Cloning, however, has its limitations. The problems of working with disease resistance in inbred strains would be even more severe when dealing with whole stands of genetically identical plants.

Even more exotic techniques for manipulating genes are just beginning to be explored. One example is cell fusion. In a recent experiment, nuclei from a culture of human cells were successfully introduced into plant cells. While such work is still only in the beginning stages of experimentation, it may result in practical applications for humans.

Probably the most promising modern technique for modifying the genetic makeup of domesticated organisms is genetic engineering. Because this is a very controversial field, however, it will be discussed in the last chapter.

8

What Is Evolution Doing
to the Human Race?

So far we have discussed evolution in a variety of micro-organisms, plants, and animals. But what of ourselves? Are we still subject to the forces of natural selection, or has civilization halted our evolution? This is an extremely complicated question debated by scientists and philosophers. Few concrete answers can be given, but the issue is certainly important.

Human hemogloblins provide one clear example of recent and ongoing evolutionary change in the human race. The effects of the abnormal forms of hemoglobin were mentioned earlier. People homozygous for the hemoglobin S allele suffer great disability and often die young. Hemoglobin C homozygotes are anemic and also less fit. Why then are these alleles, and others for different abnormal hemoglobins, found in high frequencies in certain human populations?

If the frequenciees of genes for defective hemoglobins in different populations are studied, an interesting relationship appears. About 20 per cent of West Africans are heterozygous for hemoglobin S, and some riverbank populations consist of 40 per cent heterozygotes. In one area of

Ghana, 27 per cent of the people are hemoglobin C heterozygotes. Other defective hemoglobins are common in Med-
iterranean countries. The areas where such abnormal
hemoglobins are found are also regions where malaria is
common. Malaria is caused by a microscopic parasite which
multiplies inside red blood cells. It is a very serious disease
which can result in debilitating fever, chills, and anemia.
While people with normal hemoglobins are very susceptible
to malaria, defective hemoglobins usually protect against it.
In one study using human volunteers, 14 out of 15 normal
persons infected with the malarial parasite developed serious symptoms, while only two out of 15 carriers of hemoglobin S did. Such heterozygotes are said to carry sickle-cell
trait. Although scientists are not sure how these carriers are
protected, they suggest that perhaps heterozygous red blood
cells do not live as long as normal cells and therefore cannot support the full development of the malarial parasite.

Now we can understand the high frequency of defective hemoglobins in certain populations. Where malaria
occurs, normal homozygotes are susceptible to malaria and
are therefore at a disadvantage. Homozygotes for abnormal
hemoglobins are also at a disadvantage, for they have severe
anemia. But heterozygotes are resistant to malaria and are
at most mildly anemic. They therefore will have a greater
chance of having offspring than either normal or anemic
homozygotes. When the threat of malaria is removed, either
by medical advances or by immigration, the frequency of
abnormal hemoglobins declines. Scientists estimate that at
least 22 per cent of slaves brought to America carried the
sickle-cell trait. The combination of lowered selection pressure for the sickle-cell trait and gene exchange with whites
and other groups has lowered the frequency of sickle-cell

People with sickle-cell disease have misshapen red blood cells, often of a more or less sickle shape. Normal cells, seen below, go through small blood vessels easily, but the sickle cells cause clogging, with anemia and deterioration of various organs resulting. The same genes that cause sickling protect the carrier of them against malaria, however.

trait among present-day American Blacks to about 10 per cent. Even so, sickle-cell anemia is a serious problem in our country as well as in Africa. About 40,000 American Blacks today have the disease. Their life expectancy is less than 20 years, and they live those years in pain and ill health. Only recently have doctors turned their attention to serious study of sickle-cell anemia. Now Black couples can learn through genetic counseling if they risk having a child with this disease, and new methods of treatment are easing the suffering of its victims.

Human Blood Groups

We begin to see how complicated the process of evolution is. Human blood groups provide an example of possible opposing selection pressures in humans, leading to the maintenance of several alleles of one gene in the population. When more than one allele is common in a population the gene in question is said to be polymorphic—having a number of different forms. Several polymorphisms for blood proteins are known in human beings. The best known is the ABO polymorphism, which is important in matching blood types for transfusions.

A 1970 survey showed that various diseases have different frequencies among different blood types. For example, one kind of influenza occurs 22 per cent more often among type O persons than among type A, while A persons are 27 per cent more likely to get acute hepatitis than are O persons. Blood-group frequencies are also related to different disease epidemics. There are fewer O individuals in areas where the dreaded bubonic plague was once common. Places where severe outbreaks of smallpox occurred have fewer

A people. Although scientists do not yet agree on the reasons for these correlations of blood type with disease, natural selection is certainly involved, both in the proportion of different blood groups in these populations and in maintaining the polymorphism.

Selection Pressures Today

Modern city life is very different from the lives of our ancestors. The social and emotional pressures on people are bound to have evolutionary results. Marriage among different races and nationalities has increased in the modern world, leading to greater heterozygosity in a segment of the human race. Increased exposure to radiation and certain drugs has increased the mutation rate of the human species. Although we cannot measure the effects of these and other changes in our genetic endowment, we should realize that humanity is not genetically stable.

A serious question posed by many concerned persons today, laymen and scientists alike, is the effect of modern medicine on the fitness of present and future human populations. Only a few generations ago, half the humans born died before reaching reproductive age. There were various causes, ranging from birth defects to infectious diseases. Today many diseases have been conquered and victims of many birth defects can be saved from death. By rescuing such presumably weak individuals, do we weaken the human race? While few persons question the moral necessity of doing what we can to insure the best possible health for humans once they are born, many people do worry about the results of this practice for our evolutionary future.

Certainly civilization has relaxed the selection pressures on human populations. In western countries most persons have children before they die; at death they have already made their contribution to the gene pool of the next generation. Susceptibility to certain diseases, such as tuberculosis, has some genetic basis. Because we can now cure this disease, persons who might have died from it are passing their susceptibility on to their children. Other diseases with a hereditary component, such as diabetes, can be managed by modern medicine so that its victims can lead a normal family life, perpetuating genes which in the old days would have been eliminated. Since there are many such "bad genes" which used to be selected against but now are maintained, certain persons believe mankind is going rapidly downhill. For example, this is a quotation from the Nobel Prize-winning geneticist H. J. Muller, writing about the future of the human race:

> Instead of people's time and energy being mainly spent in the struggle with external enemies of a primitive kind such as famine, climatic difficulties, and wild beasts, they would be devoted chiefly to the effort to live carefully, to spare and to prop up their own feeblenesses, to soothe their inner disharmonies and, in general, to doctor themselves as effectively as possible. For everyone would be an invalid, with his own special familial twists.

This is clearly a dismal and alarming view of our future. But is it accurate? Muller's pessimism rested in part on the premise that "bad genes" are rarely or never totally recessive. He felt that even in the heterozygous state, such genes somewhat weakened the constitution of the person carrying them. Thus, as our "genetic load," or proportion of harmful genes, increased, we would become progressively more feeble. Recent evidence suggests, however, that the degree of heterozygosity in living things is much greater than was thought in Muller's day. Thus heterozygosity may well be the healthy, normal condition, even if some of the alleles are harmful.

But unfortunately we simply do not know enough about the interactions of human genes and the modern environment to make any estimates about the fitness of various genotypes. We do not know if the genes that encourage getting tuberculosis, for example, have any additional negative effects. Whether or not such genes become more or less frequent will depend on their other possible effects, and on their mutation rates. If, in modern society, such genotypes are just as fit as others and increase in frequency, there should be no cause for concern as long as prevention or treatment of the disease involved is relatively easy.

Of possibly more serious consequences is the maintenance of persons with serious genetic diseases. For example, it costs about $20,000 a year to keep a hemophiliac (a person whose blood won't clot, who therefore constantly risks bleeding to death) alive. Victims of several other genetic diseases also require constant intensive care and treatment. If the number of individuals requiring this kind of investment increases, we will be investing an ever larger share of private and public money and energy in keeping alive genetically defective individuals.

Statistics here are largely reassuring, however. If a genetic disease caused by a rare recessive gene (by far the most common type) is cured to the extent that all its sufferers will reproduce normally, it would take 40 generations (1200 years) to double the incidence of homozygotes from 1 per cent to 2 per cent of the population. Unfortunately, rare dominant traits would increase at a much faster rate, potentially doubling in one generation.

Genetic Counseling

One way to avoid increasing the incidence of deleterious genes, whether or not the symptoms are treatable, is through genetic counseling. The number of human genetic diseases is large. Fortunately, it is possible to detect the heterozygote carriers of over 60 genetic diseases. Since some of these are found more frequently in certain ethnic groups or races (for example, sickle-cell anemia in Blacks), couples who fear they may risk bearing a defective child can ask for genetic advice. Closely related persons who wish to marry may also fear that they both carry the same harmful genes.

One particularly cruel genetic disorder is Tay-Sachs disease, which causes physical and mental deterioration ending in death at two to four years of age. Tay-Sachs disease occurs especially often in persons of eastern European Jewish descent. Why this is so is debatable, but it may be due to a combination of founder effects and some heterozygote advantage. There is some evidence that carriers may have increased resistance to tuberculosis.

Through genetic counseling, some American Jewish populations have been helped to avoid this heartbreaking disease. In the Baltimore-Washington area, 8000 Jews of child-bearing age were tested in 1971 to see if they were heterozygotes. About one in 30 learned that they carried the disease, and some were married to another heterozygote. Such couples have a 25 per cent chance of bearing a doomed Tay-Sachs baby. Fortunately, it is possible to determine the genotype of the embryo. If the fetus is found to be a homo-

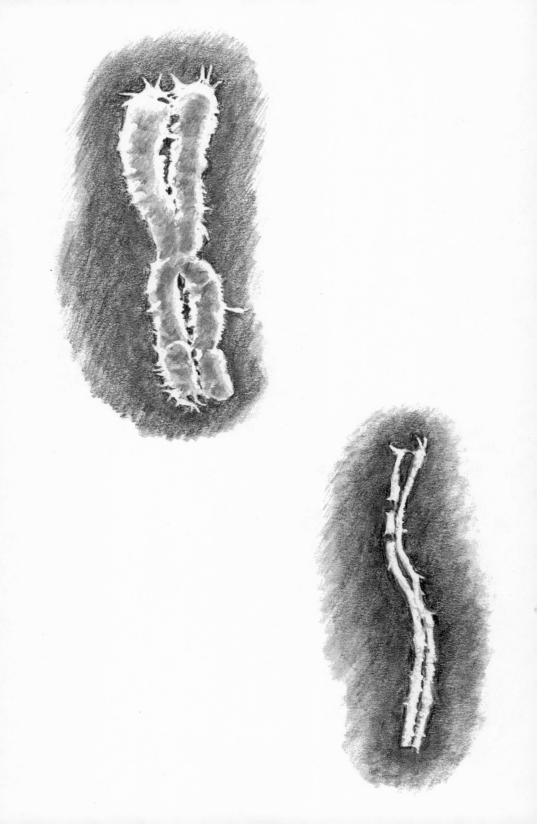

zygous recessive, the couple could decide to have a theraputic abortion rather than suffer through the certain tragedy of a deteriorating child. And if the embryo is a heterozygote or a homozygous normal, the couple can look forward with joy to the birth of a normal child.

Is Human Intelligence Declining?

Another serious question often raised these days is whether the average intelligence of the human race is decreasing through the years. The birth rate among educated persons is lower than among those with little or no education. And statistics show that the average IQ score of people from large families is lower than that of people from small families. These facts at first glance certainly appear to support the idea of declining intelligence.

But the issue is far more complicated than that. In the first place, intelligence is not a simple inherited trait. It depends partly on an interaction of many hereditary factors with environmental factors. Psychologists and biologists have yet to reach any meaningful agreement on the relative importance of these two influences. And IQ tests measure both components of intelligence. The tests are influenced

Genetic defects in humans and all organisms can come from many causes, among them atomic radiation, X-rays, ultraviolet, heat, visible light, viruses, and various chemicals. One form of chromosome damage is actual breakage of the chromosome. Top, the normal chromosome of a bean; bottom, a "naked" chromosome from a bean seedling irradiated with X-rays; two distinct breaks are seen. These pictures are based on electron-microscope pictures by two German biologists, W. Scheid and H. Traut.

by such things as skill with words, emotional state, and family stability. A change for the better in a child's environment can improve his IQ by 20 points, so the environment has considerable effect on IQ scores. We have no way of knowing for sure whether the lower IQ of persons from large families is inherited or not. As a matter of fact, a recent theory accounts very well for such differences on a purely environmental basis.

In addition, there is no evidence that poorer people without a college education are in any meaningful way "less intelligent" than college-educated people. IQ tests are the chief measure of intelligence, and we have just seen that IQ is strongly affected by both heredity and environment. No one really knows just what is measured by IQ tests, beyond the ability to succeed in an educated, white, middle-class environment. Other traits and abilities useful to society, such as creativity or mechanical ability, are not measured by these tests.

A variety of skills and talents are required in any human popuplation to keep it going. We need scientists, carpenters, bank presidents, typists, mailmen, artists, athletes, bus drivers, and so forth. Not only is it virtually impossible to measure the overall mental ability of human populations, but such a measurement would have little meaning in our complex society. Thus even the newer IQ tests which are designed to be less culture-bound than previous ones will not give us the information needed to answer our question.

The human secret of success lies in our great adaptability and flexibility as well as in our intelligence. People can live in the jungle or the big city, along the Equator or in the Arctic Circle. The variety of human types maintains that flexibility, which we will need tomorrow even more than today.

Cultural Evolution, the Special Shaper

The flexibility of what we now call the human species has largely freed it from the forces of new biological evolution and natural selection. Most of the changes in the human way of life over the time recorded by written history and the many millennia just before it occurred by cultural evolution rather than biological evolution. Human offspring have amazing flexibility, whatever their racial or cultural origin. They adopt the language, culture, and knowledge of their particular homeland and are capable of continued learning throughout their lifetimes.

Cultural evolution has several advantages over biological evolution. Its flexibility enables humans to adapt quickly to new environments, and cultural changes can be rapidly transmitted through a population by spoken and written words, by images and various art forms. Thus cultural evolution allows for more rapid adaptation than does biological evolution. Through cultural evolution, a few especially successful individuals can affect large numbers of their fellow humans, whereas through biological evolution they can affect only their own offspring.

Cultural evolution frees us from the chance nature of biological evolution. We can make deliberate changes in order to arrive at a predetermined goal. We can master many environments by finding out ways to solve problems of agriculture and husbandry, industry, commerce, and so on, and by then teaching these ways to other humans. Cultural evolution has enabled the human species to achieve its present dominant position among the earth's living things.

9

Arguing Out Evolution

Evolutionary biology today is full of controversy. There is the continuing struggle over the teaching of evolution in schools. There are disagreements among scientists over the application of evolutionary biology to the social sciences. There is controversy over the safety of certain evolutionary experiments being carried out and concern about the possibility of genetic engineering in humans. And finally, there is a great deal of disagreement among evolutionary biologists themselves over the relative importance of various factors in the course of evolution, both in the past and present.

We will not consider the moral and religious questions involved in the struggle over teaching evolution in schools. They are beyond the scope of biology. But a knowledge of evolution is necessary to understanding the life sciences. Evolution is the thread uniting all branches of biology, for the behavior, color, shape, size, and inner functioning of organisms are all, at bottom, evolutionary adaptations. Ecology is really the study of how organisms have evolved together with the result that they are able to share the earth. Without an understanding of evolution, the basic unity of life is difficult to appreciate. And the practical application of evolutionary principles is vitally important in agriculture, animal breeding, and medicine.

Sociobiology—A Controversial New Approach

The focus of a great controversy in scientific circles these days is a book published in 1975 by Professor Edward O. Wilson of Harvard University called *Sociobiology*. In it Dr. Wilson established a new field of science which integrates psychology, animal behavior, sociology, and evolutionary biology. His goal is to study social phenomena as they exist in all organisms, and only a small part of his book is devoted to speculations about the biological fundamentals of human social arrangements.

A group of scientists, including several of Dr. Wilson's Harvard colleagues, call themselves the Sociobiology Study Group of Science for the People. They object strongly to Dr. Wilson's approach to the study of humanity. They feel that any claim for an effect of human biology on human society will be used by reactionary political forces to justify social injustices. In their minds, the danger exists of people saying, for example, that since biology helps make humans aggressive and selfish, it's all right for people to be that way. They go so far as to say it is immoral even to study or write about the influences of our evolutionary history on society.

On the other hand, Dr. Wilson and his supporters feel that an understanding of the biological mechanisms at the root of human behavior will help us to understand ourselves and thereby increase our ability to improve society. They agree with the great evolutionary biologist Theodosius Dobzhansky when he wrote: "Man's future inexorably depends on the interactions of biological and social forces.

Understanding these forces and their interactions may, in the fullness of time, prove to be the main achievement of science."

Genetic Engineering and Recombinant DNA: Danger Ahead?

The subject of genetic engineering is of more immediate concern to most biologists than the the the sociobiology controversy, for today scientists have the ability to tamper radically with evolution. Genetic material from one species can be introduced into cells of another. One method for doing this is by cell fusion, in which the nucleus of one kind of cell is introduced into a different kind of cell, as briefly described in Chapter 7. Another way is through the use of plasmids. These are circles of double-stranded bacterial DNA which can be introduced into cells and will multiply there. They can exist separately from the bacterial chromosome, and carry from 15 to 200 genes. The R factors discussed in Chapter 6 are one kind of plasmid. Scientists are currently working on techniques to make plasmids carry particular pieces of DNA which can then be introduced into other cells. The hybrid DNA produced is called recombinant DNA.

In a typical experiment, a plasmid carrying a gene for resistance to the antibiotic tetracycline is used. The plasmids are treated with an enzyme which cuts the DNA molecule and opens up the circle of DNA. The desired DNA is added and is taken in by the plasmids. Certain genes occur in thousands of copies in nuclei. These genes can be isolated for transfer by plasmids. Since most genes are present in single copies, they can be transferred only by "shotgunning"

—breaking up all the genes with enzymes and brewing that DNA with the recipient plasmids. Next, the plasmids are added to the bacterial culture under conditions which will allow them to "transform" the bacterial host cells. In transformation, the bacteria take up the plasmids, which can then reproduce inside the bacteria.

Since bacterial cells which have been transformed will be resistant to tetracycline, the cells are cultured in the presence of the antibiotic so that only transformed cells can grow. After a shotgun experiment, it is also necessary to single out, perhaps by gene-function tests, the bacterial cells which contain the desired gene.

If precise methods for transferring desired genes and for getting them to function inside the bacterial cell can be worked out, the potential practical applications are enormous. For example, if the gene for the production of insulin could be introduced into easily cultured bacterial cells, large quantities of that vital hormone could be produced cheaply. Other important protein hormones, such as human growth hormone, are available in such minute quantities today that they can be used to treat only a few people. If recombinant DNA is used, these compounds could become available to anyone who needed them. Certain drugs could also be inexpensively produced with this technique.

If recombinant-DNA methods can be developed for use in plant and animal cells, even more startling practical applications could result. Plants could be induced through directed genetic change to produce higher-quality proteins and vitamins for human consumption. This would ease the increasing starvation due to the population explosion. Genetic diseases, especially those due to malformation of particular enzymes, might be corrected by introducing the

The bacillus Escherichia coli, *normally found in human intestines, is seen here attacked by viruses, which enter it, multiply inside, and cause it to burst, releasing increased numbers of viruses.* E. Coli *is used widely in recombinant-DNA experiments.*

gene for the normal enzyme molecule into the patients' cells.

Unfortunately, there are serious problems involved with recombinant-DNA experiments. Many scientists and other citizens fear that by introducing foreign genes into bacteria, strains of very dangerous microorganisms might be produced. They question the wisdom of combining DNA which would never be brought together in nature. The chief organism used in recombinant-DNA studies is the bacterium *Escherichia coli* (abbreviated *E. coli*), which is a normal inhabitant of the human intestine. Weakened strains of *E. coli* are used in the experiments. But although these strains cannot survive for long in humans, the genes they acquire through recombinant experiments, especially in shotgun experiments, could conceivably allow them to thrive outside the laboratory. Dr. Erwin Chargaff, one of the pioneers of DNA research, states these fears clearly: "You cannot recall a new form of life. Once you have constructed a viable *E. coli* cell carrying a plasmid DNA into which a piece of eukaryotic DNA [DNA from higher organisms] has been spliced, it will survive you and your children and your children's children."

Most recombinant-DNA research is paid for by the government through research grants from the National Institutes of Health (NIH). After a great deal of study and discussion, the NIH has produced guidelines designed to insure the safety of recombinant-DNA experiments. The possible types of experiments are divided into four catagories. Those called "P1" experiments are considered safe enough to conduct in any laboratory, while "P4" experiments are allowed in only certain strictly controlled laboratories. The requirements for P2 and P3 experiments are between these two extremes.

Many people are not convinced that the NIH guidelines are adequate. And they feel the public should have a greater say in determining where and how potentially dangerous experiments should be carried out. The organization Science for the People has received the support of the Cambridge, Massachusetts city council in its attempts to get more public participation in such decisions. Harvard University received permission from NIH to remodel some of its biology facilities into a P3 (moderate-containment) laboratory. But in July 1976 the Cambridge city council voted for a three-month moratorium on recombinant-DNA research within the Cambridge city limits while it studies the prickly and highly technical questions involved.

Other Recombinant-DNA Research

Other, less controversial approaches are also being used to study ways of transferring DNA from one organism to another. One experiment involved soaking embryos of laboratory fruit flies in a DNA solution or injecting them with DNA. The recipient embryos were homozygous recessives for an easily recognizable trait, colorless eyes, while the donor DNA was dominant normal. A few of the flies which developed had normally colored eyes (too many to have resulted from mutations), showing that the embryonic cells were capable of taking up DNA from the outside. It is also possible to add wild-type DNA of the bread mold Neurospora to the growth medium of a mutant culture and "cure" the mutation.

In studies of the crown gall disease of plants, evidence has been found that bacterial DNA may be transferred in nature to plant cells and reproduce there. Crown gall is

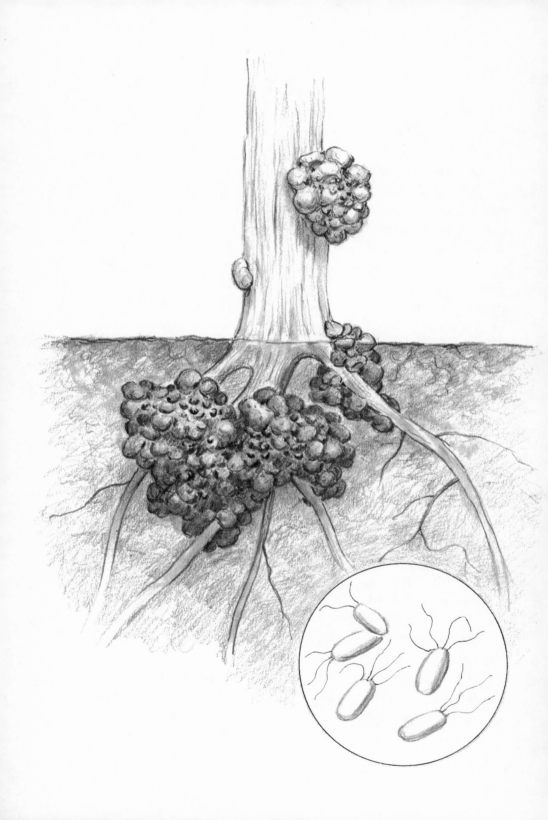

caused by a bacterium and results in tumors of several plant species. Scientists have found evidence that DNA from plasmids of the infecting bacteria is present in plant tumor cells. If the tumor cells are grown in culture, the bacterial DNA remains for several decades. The natural barrier against combining bacterial DNA with that from higher organisms may not be as close to absolute as was previously thought.

Genetic Engineering in Humans

Peering into the future, some people see frightening possibilities for the misuse of genetic knowledge in the human race. They fear that genetic engineering could be used to transform men and women by using "bad" genes as well as "good" genes. They fear the possibility that techniques might be developed to clone humans like carrots or pine trees to produce an army of geniuses or madmen. Such speculations are beyond the scope of this book, for they are moral and political questions more than biological ones. Two books, Daniel S. Halacy's *Genetic Revolution* and Carl Heintze's *Genetic Engineering*, discuss these and other aspects of modern genetics more thoroughly.

Natural Selection and Genetic Drift

Throughout this book the importance of natural selection in evolution has been emphasized. No evolutionary

Crown gall disease produces tumors on plants, especially just below ground. It is caused by the bacteria shown encircled. DNA from plasmids of these bacteria enters the tumor cells, a fact that is important to recombinant-DNA researchers.

biologist denies that natural selection has been a vital force throughout the history of life on earth. But many scientists today have concluded that genetic drift is far more important than was previously believed, especially in the evolution of population differences which lead eventually to new species. Other scientists stoutly defend the role of natural selection, saying that just because we don't know the selective advantage of a certain allele, that doesn't mean there is no such advantage.

The study of molecular genetics has provided a lot of new information about genetic variability in natural populations. Molecular genetics investigates amino acid differences in proteins from different populations and species. Mutations are changes in the base sequence of the DNA molecule leading to amino acid substitutions in proteins. Because the electrical charge of different amino acids varies, some of the acid substitutions will result in a change in the electrical charge of the protein molecule. These changes in charge can be detected through a technique called electrophoresis.

In this technique the proteins are placed in solution in an electrical field and their relative movements in the field are noted. If two versions of the protein in question (called allozymes) have different charges, they will move at different rates in the field. The allozymes are products of the genes, so genetic variability can be measured right at the level of the alleles, rather than through some further removed visible characteristic such as eye color or hair texture.

Many scientists were surprised by the results of such protein studies. They expected little variability in the protein products of each gene. But in most populations, at least 30 per cent of genes of sexually reproducing animals have more than one allele. And any one individual will have two different alleles present for about 10 per cent of its genes. These facts argue strongly against H. J. Muller's classical model of genetics. Dr. Muller thought that almost all individuals of one species would carry the same alleles for each gene. He called these the "wild-type" alleles. Muller's pessimism about the future of the human race was based on his belief that heterozygotes were generally less fit than homozygous "wild-type" individuals. Apparently he was wrong, since every individual seems to carry alternate alleles for at least some genes.

Other scientists, such as Dr. Theodosius Dobzhansky, believed that there must be great genetic variability for natural selection to act upon. Their theory is called the "balance theory," for it sees genetic variability as a dynamic thing. Different alleles are selected under different circumstances, and those individuals carrying different alleles for the same gene would have an advantage rather than a disadvantge.

Believers in the balance school were not surprised to see the great genetic variability revealed by electrophoresis. But believers in the classical theory were dismayed. How could there be so much genetic variability without the genetic load and the rate of evolution being too great? They have figured a very simple way out of this. They say that the variability in protein molecules is not really the point in evolution, for it is selectively neutral. They feel that small differences in protein molecules cannot be detected by natural selection and therefore that varying forms of proteins are due to genetic drift.

Most variations in human hemoglobins are considered by these scientists to be selectively neutral. Some mutant hemoglobins, such as the one causing sickle-cell anemia, are far from neutral. But many others appear to function just like normal hemoglobins. Although scientists debating the issue of neutral traits are talking about protein differences, we can easily think of visible differences which might be selectively neutral. Spotted skunks show a great variety of coat patterns. As long as the basic warning black and white are present, it seems the precise arrangement of spots should make little difference. In humans, natural selection has been relaxed sufficiently that variations in such traits as hair color, eyelash length, nose shape and so forth could be selectively neutral.

But we must always be careful in discussing the neutrality of visible traits, for they are produced by the interaction of the genes and the environment; they are not the direct products of genes. In addition, many genes have more than one effect. Nose shape might be affected by genes which influence the growth of the whole skeleton in important ways. The fact that most visible traits are affected by more than one gene is a further complicating factor.

The major evidence for the neutrality theory comes from studies of changes in the amino acid sequences in related organisms. There appears to be an "evolutionary clock" ticking away once new species of animals have gone their own way. The blood proteins of animals such as mammals (which evolved fairly recently—about 75 million years ago) are more similar to each other than are the blood proteins of frogs, which have been around for about 150 million years. The changes are related to the length of time species have lived apart rather than to their differences in size and shape or way of life.

There is also evidence to support the balance hypothesis. Several studies have found important relationships between states of the environment and allele frequencies in a variety of organisms. The set-to between supporters of the neutrality theory and the balance hypothesis will continue for years before enough evidence is gathered to determine the relative importance of selection and drift.

Evolution and Changes in Gene Regulation

Scientists assumed for many years that the differences between species, especially strikingly different ones, were due to the accumulation of many small gene differences. According to this idea, the effects of all these small differences within the organism add up to large differences between organisms. With the advent of electrophoretic studies and other modern techniques for uncovering the genetic similarity between organisms, a startling result has emerged. *Dissimilar* species may be strikingly *similar* in their genetic endowment.

The best example of this phenomen is a comparison between humans and chimpanzees. The differences in body form and psychology between the two species are undeniably very great. Chimps and humans are placed by zoologists in different families because they seem so dissimilar. But 44 proteins of chimps and humans proved on the average to be 99 per cent identical. The DNA of the two is also very much alike. By these criteria, chimps and ourselves are as closely related as fruit fly species which look virtually identical. Then why are the two species so different?

The answer seems to lie in the great importance of gene regulation during animal development and afterward. For example, if the forces regulating brain growth shut it off at an earlier stage of development in one species than in another, the effects on the whole life of the animal will be tremendous.

Such changes can be brought about by single mutations in regulatory genes. However, such key mutations are not the whole story. Changes in the chromosomes are also involved. We do not yet understand gene regulation and the significance of the order of genes along the chromosome in higher organisms. But more chromosome changes, such as those in number and shape of chromosomes, are found between members of animal classes (such as mammals) which have evolved more rapidly than among those (such as frogs) which have evolved more slowly. This evidence strengthens the argument mentioned earlier that proteins evolve at a more constant rate which is not closely matched with the evolutionary rate.

Changes in chromosome rearrangement are known to be important in developing new species of organisms such as fruit flies. And studies conducted over many years have shown regular ups and downs in the frequencies of different chromosome arrangements within a fruit fly species according to the season, suggesting that the rearrangements do in some way relate to important genetic differences.

In recent years our ideas about evolution have needed some revising, and perhaps even more revision is in the making.

Non-Mendelian Inheritance

One factor which may have more importance in evolution than most scientists have realized is non-Mendelian inheritance. Although most of the DNA of higher organisms is present in nuclear chromosomes, some exist, in the cytoplasm, the cell material that is outside the nucleus. Many examples exist of traits controlled by extranuclear DNA. Such characteristics are often hard to study, for in order to detect the existence of the trait in the first place, there must be some sort of mutant phenotype which can be distinguished from the wild type. Also, such traits are transmitted only by the mother to the offspring through the egg cytoplasm in most cases, and therefore scientists cannot follow the segregation of the genes in succeeding generations. Examples of inheritance controlled by genes outside the nucleus include shell-coiling in snails, streptomycin resistance in a single-celled alga, eye color in beach hoppers (a type of amphipods, which are small crustaceans), and a breast-cancer-producing virus in mouse milk.

Such independent genes may be present in chloroplasts and mitochondria and are very important from an evolutionary point of view. Chloroplasts are found in green plants. They contain the chemical chlorophyll, which enables them to trap the energy of the sun and use it to convert carbon dioxide and water into sugars. Chloroplasts contain some DNA which controls some of their traits. Other chloroplast traits are controlled by genes in the nucleus.

Mitochondria are particles in the cytoplasm which provide energy for the cell. Higher plant and animals cells cannot live and grow without them. The mitochondria of some organisms, such as yeasts, contain 10 to 20 per cent of the total cellular DNA. Yeasts with faulty mitochondrial DNA cannot reproduce sexually and can grow and divide only weakly. Mitochondrial genes have been shown to control some traits of mitochondria, and these genes are independent of the nucleus.

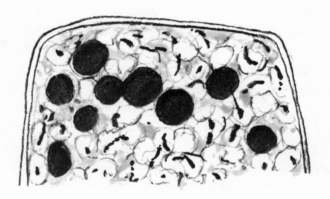

Chloroplasts (dark discs) in a plant cell contain chlorophyll, necessary in manufacturing food for the plant; the black threads and dots are mitochondria, in which respiration occurs and energy is generated. The mitochondria of some organisms contain DNA which is not inside the cell's nucleus; chloroplasts too contain nonnuclear DNA.

Many scientists today believe that chloroplasts and mitochondria have evolved from originally independent organisms which became associated during evolution with the ancestors of true cells. Very gradually the chloroplasts and mitochondria became more dependent on the cells and vice versa, until neither could survive without the other. This interesting idea is explored in detail by Lynn Margulis (see Suggested Reading).

Inheritance of Acquired Characteristics

The vast majority of biologists today believe that inheritance of acquired characteristics does not occur. They feel that mutation and natural selection, combined with the influence of other factors such as chance, can explain all evolutionary events, given the tremendous span of time from the origin of life on earth to today.

A very few scientists believe in the possibility that some sort of feedback system from the environment to the genes is possible, causing appropriate gene changes which could be passed on to the next generation.

The DNA of genes is associated with particular proteins. Recent studies have shown that most nuclear DNA is present in segments of 180 to 200 subunits, each segment being associated with particular proteins. The segments are arranged in a line, one after another. The DNA of an active gene appears to be different in some way from that of an inactive one, and researchers believe that the difference lies in the way the DNA and the protein are combined. The cellular environment can cause temporary gene changes, turning genes on and off, depending on the current needs of the cell. The few scientists who believe in the possibility of inheritance of acquired characteristics feel that perhaps the environment could cause permanent as well as temporary gene changes through proteins associated with genes.

This viewpoint is a very unpopular one, because it goes against the current unified concept of heredity and evolution. Definitive experiments have yet to be done which could demonstrate this kind of gene change, though claims of showing proof have been made.

If definitive experiments are ever performed, it is to be hoped that the scientific community will give them the kind of consideration they would deserve. Biologists have been very wrong before. Prior to the 1950s, for example, most researchers were convinced that the DNA molecule was too simple to be the hereditary material. And when non-chromosomal DNA was found in mitochondria and chloroplasts, it was a long time before some prominent scientists accepted its existence. Scientists of all people must make an effort to keep an open mind and be willing to modify their theories and opinions. We still have a lot to learn about the history of life on earth, and may be in for some big surprises as we learn more and more about evolution. Like evolving species, our ideas about the process are evolving too.

Glossary

alleles   Variations of the same gene.

allozymes   Different forms of the same enzyme, having some difference in amino acid sequence.

attenuation   The weakening of a disease-organism strain so that it no longer causes serious illness.

chromosome   A structure present in the nucleus which contains the genes; can be seen during cell division.

clone   A population of organisms with identical genetic endowment.

code for   "Give orders" for the structure of proteins, and thus for traits; DNA is said to code for one protein or another.

coevolution   Evolution of species as they interact with and adapt to one another.

cytoplasm   The cell material that is outside the nucleus.

DNA   The chemical that genes are made of; contains the "genetic code."

dominant allele   An allele which produces its phenotypic effect even if a different allele is present on the homologous chromosome.

founder effect   A chance shift in gene frequency of a population due to the small number of first "settlers" of the new population.

gene   The unit of inheritance; usually defined today as the length of DNA that codes for a particular protein.

gene frequency   The proportion of a certain allele in a particular population.

gene pool   All the alleles of all genes present in a population of organisms.

generation time The length of time from birth to reproduction in a particular species.

genetic drift Changes in gene frequencies due to chance rather than to selection.

genetic load The proportion of "bad" alleles which are carried along in a population.

genotype The genetic endowment of an organism.

genus (pl., *genera*) A category consisting of closely related species; placed as the first scientific name of a species.

heterozygote An organism with two different alleles of a particular gene.

homologous chromosomes The two chromosomes of a pair, carrying the same genes.

homozygote An organism with the same allele of a certain gene present on both homologous chromosomes.

horizontal resistance Resistance to plant diseases due to an accumulation of small effects; usually effective against many pest strains, though not all.

locus (pl., *loci*) The position on a chromosome occupied by a particular gene. In genetic discussion it often is used interchangeably with the word "gene."

meiosis Cell division that forms the egg and sperm cells, during which the chromosome number is halved.

mitosis Cell division in which the chromosomes are duplicated exactly, forming two identical "daughter" cells.

N The number of differing chromosome pairs of a species; body cells of higher organisms contain 2N chromosomes; egg and sperm cells have 1N chromosomes.

niche The way of life of a particular species, including what it eats, where it lives, what enemies it has, and so forth.

parthenogenetic development Egg development without fertilization.

phenotype The "appearance" of an organism; caused by the interaction of genotype and environment.

plasmid A circle of DNA carrying genes which can be transferred from one bacterium to another; plasmids have so far been found only in bacteria and can exist outside the chromosome.

polymer A chemical molecule consisting of a repeating series of similar or identical smaller units of relatively simple molecules.

polymorphic gene A gene with more than one allele in a certain population.

recessive allele An allele which is expressed phenotypically only when it is present on both homologous chromosomes.

selection pressure A force favoring evolution in a certain direction.

speciation The process of species formation.

species A group of potentially interbreeding organisms usually well isolated reproductively from other species.

vertical resistance Disease resistance in plants due usually to a single dramatic effect; often not effective against all pest strains.

virulence The ability of a disease organism to cause disease; a virulent strain causes serious illness.

Suggested Reading

Books

Isaac Asimov, *The Genetic Code* (Orion Press, N.Y., 1962)
Charles Darwin, *The Voyage of the Beagle*, abridged by Millicent E. Selsam (Harper and Row, N.Y., 1959)
Alice Dickenson, *Charles Darwin and Natural Selection* (Watts, N.Y., 1964)
D. S. Halacy, *Genetic Revolution: Shaping Life for Tomorrow* (Harper and Row, N.Y., 1975)
Carl Heintze, *Genetic Engineering: Man and Nature in Transition* (Thomas Nelson and Co., N.Y., 1974)
Ruth Moore, *Evolution* (Time-Life, N.Y., 1964)
Frank H. T. Rhodes, *Evolution: A Golden Guide* (Golden/Western, N.Y., 1974)

This is just a sampling of the books available on evolution.

Magazine Articles

Anthony C. Allison, "Sickle Cells and Evolution," *Scientific American*, Aug. 1956
J. A. Bishop and Laurence M. Cook, "Moths, Melanism, and Clean Air," *Scientific American*, Jan. 1975
Luigi Luca Cavalli-Sforga, " 'Genetic Drift' in an Italian Population," *Scientific American*, Aug. 1969

Anthony Cerami and Charles M. Peterson, "Cyanate and Sickle-Cell Disease," *Scientific American*, April 1975

Bryan Clarke, "The Causes of Biological Diversity," *Scientific American*, Aug. 1975 (Diversity and natural selection in snails today)

Royston Clowes, "The Molecule of Infectious Drug Resistance," *Scientific American*, April 1973 (Detailed discussion of R factors)

Stanley N. Cohen, "The Manipulation of Genes," *Scientific American*, July 1975

Theodosius Dobzhansky, "The Present Evolution of Man," *Scientific American*, Sept. 1960

Niles Eldredge, "Survivors from the Good Old, Old, Old Days," *Natural History*, Feb. 1975 (About species which have evolved little and why)

Michael Gruber and John Shoup, "Crabs Move Ashore," *Sea Frontiers*, Nov-Dec. 1969

Robert S. O. Harding and Shirley C. Strum, "Predatory Baboons of Kekopey," *Natural History*, March 1976 (Rapid evolution of meat-eating behavior)

Paul A. Johnsgard, "Natural and Unnatural Selection in a Wild Goose," *Natural History*, Dec. 1973 (Effects of humans on evolution of blue and snow goose)

Lynn Margulis, "Symbiosis and Evolution," *Scientific American*, Aug. 1971

Roger Tory Peterson, "The Galapagos, Eerie Cradle of New Species," *National Geographic*, April 1967

Francis J. Ryan, "Evolution Observed," *Scientific American*, Oct. 1953

G. Ledyard Stebbins, "Cataclysmic Evolution," *Scientific American*, April 1951

Gary S. Stein, Janet Swinehart Stein, and Lewis J. Kleinsmith, "Chromosomal Proteins and Gene Regulation," *Scientific American*, Feb. 1975

Alan Villiers, "In the Wake of Darwin's Beagle," *National Geographic*, Oct. 1969

Emile Zuckerkandl, "Evolution of Hemoglobin," *Scientific American*, May 1965 (Lots of biochemistry in this one)

See also the column "Bios," by Arthur W. Galston, in *Natural History*, which often deals with evolutionary topics. Examples: "Molding New Plants," Nov. 1974; "Here Come the Clones," Feb. 1975

The column "This View of Life," by Stephen J. Gould, also in *Natural History*, concerns evolutionary topics as well. Example: "A Threat to Darwinism," Dec. 1975, deals with the neutralist controversy.

Index

38195

J
575 P
PATENT
    EVOLUTION GOES ON EVERY DAY
        6.95